We

*Ditch the Me Mindset
and Change the World*

We

Ditch the Me Mindset and Change the World

By
Eric George, M.D.

Todd Stansfield, *Editor*
Susan Strecker, *Associate Editor*
Audra Gerber, *Copy Editor*

MAGNUSSON-SKOR
PUBLISHING, LLC

Published by

MAGNUSSON-SKOR
PUBLISHING, LLC

Magnusson-Skor Publishing
4600 S. Ulster Street, Suite 1450, Denver, CO 80237
www.mskor.com
Copyright © 2019 by Magnusson-Skor Publishing, LLC
Cover design by The Book Designers

Library of Congress Control Number: 2019901237

ISBN: 9780999888834

First Edition

CONTENTS

CONTENTS

ABOUT *the* AUTHOR

Eric R. George, M.D., is a renowned hand surgeon, serial entrepreneur, venture capitalist, and philanthropist. He is the founder and CEO of Omega Hospital, New Orleans's first physician-owned hospital; the Hand Center of Louisiana, where he actively practices; and ERG Enterprises, a $500 million investment firm committed to changing communities worldwide.

In addition to practicing medicine full-time, he owns and operates businesses in numerous industries, such as hospitality, real estate, oil and gas, education, entertainment, and consumer goods. As a philanthropist, he established the Colonel Aaron C-Dot George Scholarship at Marshall University, an annual fund named after his brother who died as a fighter pilot in a training accident. He also serves on numerous civic, charitable, and educational boards, and contributes to many causes, including the New York University School of Law, the St. Martin's Episcopal School George Cottage in New Orleans, and a school for orphans in Mombasa, Kenya.

Dr. George credits his success and balance to the talented and caring individuals around him, who share his passion for meeting and helping others, as well as his loving wife, Kim, and two daughters, Chloe and Cassidy.

ACKNOWLEDGMENTS

John Donne once wrote, "No man is an island, entire of itself; every man is a piece of a continent, a part of the main." His writings speak of a universal reality. Success doesn't depend on individual greatness alone, but rather from collective participation, support, and coordination. In other words, we can't accomplish anything remarkable without the help of others, a reason I would like to acknowledge several important people for their impact on my life.

First, I would like to praise Kim, my wife of almost 30 years, for acting as my foundation and balancing force; and my daughters, Chloe and Cassidy, for enriching my life and challenging me to become a better father, husband, person, and professional. Additionally, I would like to show my appreciation to my father for his invaluable mentorship and encouragement, and my mother for her continual care and support. Likewise, I want to recognize Anthony, my older brother, for his timely advice over the years, and Ethan, my younger brother, for his exceptional positivity. I would also like to thank Brandin Cooks for his energy and enthusiasm, and for bringing me into his life.

I would be remiss if I didn't recognize the people who support my work as a hand surgeon and entrepreneur. To this end,

I would like to call out Craig Henry, my office manager at the Hand Center of Louisiana, for his daily contributions to growing our practice. I also want to acknowledge everyone at the Hand Center for their tireless efforts.

Outside of practicing medicine, I want to say thank you to Barrett Cooper, my chief financial officer (CFO) at ERG Enterprises, for helping me establish ERG as a successful investment capital company. I would like to extend my appreciation to the entire team at ERG, where I am continually impressed by the exceptional talent, hard work, and commitment I see daily.

This list would not be complete without acknowledging the contributions of Jerry Marty, the longtime CFO of many of my companies. Jerry has been instrumental to my success, and to his credit, he remains one of the humblest people I know.

There are many others deserving of recognition who are not named here, but who nonetheless remain integral to my life. To each, I would like to say thank you.

Last, I would like to acknowledge Todd Stansfield, who was integral to the writing of this book. Thank you for introducing me to the joy of storytelling.

PREFACE

I sat in my study and puzzled over one of the more difficult tasks of writing this book. I needed to craft a title that would encompass the philosophy that continues to enrich my life. Given all that I wanted to say and everything I believed about connectedness, I struggled. It finally occurred to me days after beginning the exercise. Lost in the many scribbles and musings scattered across my desk, I found one word that captured the essence of my thinking: *We*. I immediately saw it as an apt and fitting title for this work. It encompassed the simplicity of my message while also paying homage to the essential condition of collaboration.

This book presents a lifestyle and mindset that continues to inform how I approach everything from my family to my businesses to my patients. It speaks to a core set of beliefs that centers on the concept of connectedness, which we examine through a series of eight chapters.

In Chapter 1, we explore the antithesis of connectedness, the mindset of "Me versus We." It remains a common point of view in life and business, and presents significant consequences. We examine these consequences in detail and uncover how this mindset manifests itself in three ways: a tendency to seek absolute independence, believe that our destiny is determined, and embrace a win-lose mindset that influences how we engage with and view others.

In Chapter 2, we review the concept of connectedness and begin our exploration of it. I use many stories from my own life to show its impact on my success, not only as a practitioner but also as an entrepreneur, father, and husband. We then review six transformative outcomes of embracing this mindset and life force, which include purpose, partnerships, perseverance, support, perspective, and trust.

Chapters 3 through 8 examine each outcome in detail, including how it contributes to a life of abundance and how connectedness reinforces it. In Chapter 3, we explore the first outcome of purpose, which enables us to find fulfillment while helping others. Chapter 4 focuses on the second outcome, partnerships, which serve as our greatest and most sustainable asset. Chapter 5 pertains to perseverance, a necessary requirement for success in any endeavor. Chapter 6 explores the fourth outcome, support, and its importance in a professional context. Chapter 7 examines the power and value of perspective in life and business. Chapter 8 focuses on trust as an essential condition to any fruitful and enduring relationship. In each chapter, we examine the outcomes through real-life anecdotes and examples.

Early into this project, I made the intentional decision to approach the work as a storyteller. I didn't want to lecture readers on the benefits of connectedness or the need to adopt this mindset. Rather, I wanted to show them how this philosophy has transformed my life and the people surrounding me. I thought, what better way to achieve this than to share my experiences? At the very least, I thought this would make the book more interesting. Yet I hoped it would provide readers with a better understanding of connectedness, its importance, and the benefits of embracing it. Using stories would also help me present readers with a new way of living, without prescribing it as the only approach. I believe the tales contained in this book accomplish these aims.

I sincerely hope that you enjoy reading this book and that it helps you find success in your personal and professional endeavors.

We

Ditch the Me Mindset and
Change the World

INTRODUCTION

We use them to greet friends, congratulate acquaintances, and embrace loved ones.

To lay bricks, perform surgeries, and sculpt artwork.

To eat, drink, and perform activities of daily living.

Everyone uses them thousands of times a day in a variety of different ways.

It took me years to recognize the essential role they play in everyone's life, no matter their age, ethnicity, or background. For someone with a passion for meeting new people, learning about them, and caring for them, they proved the perfect focus for my career.

It took a journey through medical school and two fellowships to discover that I wanted to become a hand surgeon, but since then, my decision has never wavered.

For my entire life, I have felt the need to look forward and find ways to meet and help people. The hand serves as the perfect vessel for fulfilling this need. It provides the window into a fascinating world of possibility and opportunity.

My family thinks of me as a hand surgeon; my patients refer to me as such. But truthfully, I find it difficult to put a label on the nature of my profession, because I don't fit the typical description of a practitioner. Business interests me, something that made me different from my fellow students in medical school. I like people—not to say that most physicians don't—yet I feel an insatiable curiosity to learn about their lives, perspectives, and ideas.

In many ways, the hand introduced me to the life I currently lead. It includes medicine, but also much more—a role as a caring and devoted father and husband, serial entrepreneur and investor, and philanthropist.

If you met me today, you wouldn't mistake me for an entrepreneur. Dressed in a white lab coat, notes tucked against my side, I walk briskly down the hall at the Hand Center of Louisiana, the practice for which I am the founder and CEO. My week vacillates between surgeries and hand consultations, and today will focus on meeting with the patients scheduled to see me.

Up ahead, I see my devoted staff enter an exam room. They stay a few rooms and minutes ahead of me as I make my rounds, enough time for them to take patients' histories, perform X rays, and complete anything else before I arrive. It allows everything to run smoothly so I can devote my full attention to the time I spend with each patient.

I enter my first exam room. I take a seat at the desk across from Mr. Jones, a new patient. We make small talk before discussing his symptoms. Naturally, I reach across the desk and take his injured hand in mine. I examine it carefully, knowing well the trust he places in me. I know from the notes the reason for his visit. But I ask him anyway.

"I injured it working an oil rig up north," he says.

"Oil rig? That's interesting. Tell me about that," I say.

Our conversation dovetails into everything from his work to his decision to work in oil and gas. He talks about his good fortune in finding work with his current employer, and the fear of losing his job because of his latest injury.

"Well, let's look at the X rays," I say.

Our visit ends with my recommending surgery, a procedure that should relieve what ails Mr. Jones and prevents him from pursuing his passion. We exchange pleasantries before I exit the room, into the busy hallway, and move on to start the process again. My patients come from every background imaginable—men, women, children, woodworkers, engineers, authors, and even the occasional movie star or NFL athlete.

I designed the clinic to support my life of connectedness and maximize the number of people I can meet, learn about, and care for on any given day. Every room supports the exact same configuration, down to the contents of the desk drawers and placement of office supplies, so staff always find what they need. Beside the desk, staff only need to press one of several color-coded buttons to alert their colleagues to bring patients' medication to the room. A simple action expedites the process, surprising patients and reinforcing their confidence in our ability to provide great care. The floors outside the exam room offer a wayfinding system using colored tiles that even those who are color blind can distinguish. Think how runways use lighting systems to facilitate the takeoff and landing of thousands of airplanes a day, only in this case, the floors provide guidance to hundreds of patients navigating the labyrinth of hallways and exam rooms to locate their next destination (e.g., the X-ray room or waiting area). As a result, staff spend less time directing patients where to go, patients enjoy more autonomy, and the efficiency and experience improves for all. More patients return to our clinic and refer their friends and family. Our reach and impact expands, which further allows me to connect with people from all walks.

The clinic begins to settle from its lively state as the day progresses quickly. The chatter from the waiting room recedes, as does the incessant ringing of the telephones, and the bustle of staff going room to room. I begin to hear the rumblings of the cleaning crew, a sign that it's nearing time to leave.

My phone pings me with my next appointment on the calendar. *ERG Enterprises—Board Meeting—6:00 p.m.*

I check the time, calculate for traffic, and soon head out the door to my other life.

In many ways, one could call this way of living—balancing the seemingly opposite worlds of medicine with entrepreneurship—controlled chaos. Certainly, I may have thought so before I stepped into these shoes. But once I did, I discovered all the joy and possibilities that come with it, something I continually remind myself in everything I do.

In many ways, my focus on the hand has taught me the value, importance, and benefits of embracing a mindset of "We versus Me"—a message I hope to spread and the purpose of this book.

I come across many people, in my work as a physician and entrepreneur, who say no without even considering yes. Or who say they can't because they don't know how.

My response to them would sound like this. I don't know hospitality, real estate, education, or other fascinating sectors, but nonetheless, I find myself deeply involved in these industries as an entrepreneur and investor. Had I refused the opportunities presented to me, had I confined myself to practicing medicine, I wouldn't be engaged in what I am today. I can name numerous examples of remarkable businesses that I wouldn't know if not for my constant pursuit to expand my world, including the people and possibilities within it.

My focus on the hand brought me to the dance, but my insatiable curiosity for meeting and learning from others, keeping an open mind, and understanding that we can learn any new system has kept me dancing. Today, all my business interests trace their origins to a connection I made in my journey, many in this very clinic.

I believe in the limitless power of people working together to achieve shared goals. Goals they might not know yet but that, nonetheless, can enrich their lives.

Take my recent interest in oil and gas. I knew nothing about the industry until I met someone who did, and I discovered my fascination with our ability to frack the earth and bring forth a natural resource that can power the world. Or take the hundreds of small businesses I continue to encounter, many challenging the status quo and decades-old systems too stubborn to change. None of my experiences—getting to know these unique businesses and learning how I could help fuel their impact—would exist without a mindset of We, of connectedness.

My exposure to people from all backgrounds and professions, coupled with the volume of patients I see, continues to strengthen my belief in the power of human connection. A belief that says embracing a mindset of connectedness leads to a life of abundance. Abundance, in this sense, does not simply mean making money; it can't be restricted to financial terms. It means whatever makes us feel complete, fulfilled, and successful, according to how each of us defines success. It is by no means restricted just to physicians. Anyone, in any profession and at any stage of their professional journey, can discover the value of connectedness.

My goal in writing this book is not to tell people how to live their lives but to share the experiences and philosophy that continue to help me lead an enriching one.

The origins of my life as an entrepreneur trace back to Omega Hospital. A group of physicians and I bought the hospital from a friend and colleague who was terminally ill. Omega became the first physician-owned, freestanding hospital in New Orleans and one of the first in the country. It marked my foray into entrepreneurship and leadership. I discovered how to deal with doctors, other businesses, and management. It also put me into contact with many pillars in the New Orleans community. It led to my first transition outside of health care into hospitality, soon followed by other industries. I have spent the last 26 years seeking out and developing connections, not only in industry but in every aspect of my life.

Many years and opportunities later, I find myself still practicing medicine Monday through Friday while scraping together time for my family and businesses. Along the way, I continue to encounter new challenges and requirements, but nothing proves insurmountable with a strong connection to people whom I can help and who can help me—patients and their family members, existing business partners, professional acquaintances, and anyone whose paths I cross. And most importantly, my strength comes from my strong foundation of support: Kim, my wife; Chloe and Cassidy, my daughters; my parents and brothers; and my other close relationships. Our connection removes every obstacle and enables us to achieve our goals together. For me, that means continuing to pursue my passions for medicine and business without compromise.

Throughout my journey, I discovered six key outcomes of connectedness. They continue to enrich my life personally and professionally, a reason I want to share them with you. In this book, I explore each of these outcomes in detail, including how they continue to shape my life and the lives of everyone with whom I come into contact. My sincerest hope is that by reading this book, you discover these outcomes in your life, including a new outlook that enables you to achieve success in all your endeavors.

1

The RISK *of* "ME" VERSUS "WE"

I met with a man in his early twenties named Jason, who lost his arm after getting attacked by an alligator. Jason had taunted it with fireworks, and it snuck up on him, bit his arm, dragged him into the water, and tore it off—a gruesome injury. Jason required extensive reconstructive surgery.

We sat together in the exam room for a follow-up visit, Jason sitting in the seat across from me, with his wife at his side. All the attention in the room centered on the man, whose eyes were glued to the floor. He remained unresponsive to any question his wife or I asked.

"How're you doing?" I asked several times. "How's he doing?"

He shifted his weight in his chair but didn't respond. His wife filled the silence, talking to me while looking at her husband. "He could be much better," she said. "He's given up on life, on me, our children. I don't know what to do or how to help him."

"Jason," I said. "Talk to me, pal. We can't help if you don't let us."

I spent a few more minutes trying to comfort Jason and get him to speak, but nothing seemed to take. Finally, I referred him and his wife to our counselor down the hall, a trained professional experienced in helping people like Jason accept the realities of an injury and return to some semblance of normalcy. As a standard of care, all patients visited the counselor after receiving difficult news so they could think beyond the trauma and focus on the important work ahead.

Jason's difficulties point to something I frequently see in medicine: a spirit of absolute independence. It's a mindset that, for whatever reason, makes people ignore the help readily available to them and internalize challenges, headaches, and obstacles. In medicine, I most often see it caused by trauma. Patients don't want to become a burden to family or friends. They often want to avoid thinking about their ailment altogether. Even when embracing those around them, seeking their help, and confronting their disability represents the exact solution they need. And as a result, they suffer severe depression by continually closing a crucial outlet of support.

In business, I see the destructive nature of independence manifest itself in a far different way. Entrepreneurs and aspiring professionals strive to independently achieve while ignoring the crucial relationships and resources that can help them along the way. This comes from a desire to prove their intelligence, brilliance, work ethic—whatever they consider most essential to success. Or it comes from a misplaced belief that they are the smartest or most capable person in the room. As a result, they insist on controlling all important responsibilities, constrain their people and businesses to their own capacity, and watch the great talent they have painstakingly hired leave for the competition.

Most often, I find the spirit of independence—in whatever form—to constrain people in every way and help no one in the process. Jason's independence hurt not only him but also his wife, children, and friends. Overly independent entrepreneurs not only hurt themselves, but they also hurt their employees and stakeholders as well.

After Jason left the exam room, I hoped the counselor would get through to him. Later that day, she confirmed what I feared and suspected. She, like me, wasn't successful.

A tall elderly man waved at me as I stood at the back of the line at Starbucks. Customers ahead of me turned around and stared. The man looked familiar, but I struggled to place him in my memory.

"Dr. George," he yelled. "Come up here. Let me buy you a cup of coffee."

Several people encouraged me to follow the man's directives until I joined him at the head of the line.

"Sorry, tell me your name," I said.

"Rodger," he said.

I thought for a moment. "Carpenter, right?"

"Good memory. That's me."

An older man, he appeared far more energetic and happy than he did when he first visited the clinic several years before. In fact, his life appeared to have dramatically changed since our first encounter. A woodworker by trade, he came to our clinic with a debilitating injury suffered while building a staircase for one of his clients. He lost several fingers, a common self-inflicted injury among those in his profession—so common, in fact, it carries the nickname "carpenter's finger."

On that first visit, he found the injury so devastating that he said, "I've lost my entire existence." He spoke of his craft and the more than 40 years he had devoted to it. He talked about his wife, children, and friends, how they all praised his talents for transforming a piece of wood into a cherished possession. He built homes, constructed furniture, and literally shaped how people experienced the world around them. And then all of it vanished in a fraction of a second.

"My life's over," he said at one point in the exam room, words that have stuck with me ever since.

Standing in line at the Starbucks, I realized the stark contrast between Rodger's previous and current lives. He seemed renewed, a realization that pleased me.

A barista handed him his latte. "Let me buy this," I told Rodger.

"No, no, I got it," he said. He pulled out his wallet to pay and then picked out a small picture tucked in his billfold. He handed it to me, and I looked over the photo of Rodger sitting with two small toddlers draped over his lap. All were smiling.

"Who are they?" I asked.

He teared up, and the creases in his cheeks deepened. "I'm a grandfather."

Consider Rodger's evolution from the exam room to the front of the line at Starbucks. Over time, despite the magnitude of his injury and loss of his identity, he discovered a profession far more rewarding than carpentry.

Rodger's story illustrates something common in medicine, business, and life. The weight of our present circumstances obstructs our ability to see beyond the here and now, to recognize that our circumstances, however difficult, are temporary.

It reminds me of growing up in West Virginia. I wanted to follow in the footsteps of my father and brothers, who all practiced law and whom I greatly admired. In high school, I took a placement exam to find out what career I should pursue. Unfortunately, I struggled with reading and writing, and my test scores came back below average. My teachers, who meant well, told me to consider the trades. I was devastated. Not because a career in the trades is any less important than becoming a lawyer, but it simply called into question everything I aspired to and envisioned about my life.

Like many of my patients, I felt crippled by the event.

But my parents helped me see beyond the destined path seemingly chosen for me. They encouraged me to think about college and give it a shot. I applied to Marshall University and got accepted, and much to my surprise, I began to excel. I did so well that I decided to go to medical school. And then I made another important discovery about my life, one that could have sidetracked it if not for the support of my professors and family.

In medical school, I struggled to keep pace with the tremendous volume of reading. My grades noticeably suffered, and at the end of my first year, the dean called me into his office. We carried on a long conversation about my study habits and overall performance. He couldn't understand why a student like me could struggle with reading. Later, he called Dr. Barbara Guyer, who ran the Higher Education for Learning Problems (HELP) Program at the university, to ask if she would meet with me.

Dr. Guyer administered multiple assessments. My scores on the intelligence test showed I had an IQ of 162, while a standardized assessment revealed I scored below average on reading and writing, and above average in the other disciplines, such as mathematics.

She diagnosed me with dyslexia and presented her findings to the dean. She discussed the exceptional results of my intelligence exam and recommended that I continue medical school. She also recommended that I participate in the summer HELP Program, which would teach me techniques for studying to compensate for the challenges caused by the condition. The dean agreed, and soon I entered my second year of medical school. I began to succeed, and by my fourth year, I earned straight As.

I eventually applied to a fellowship at Michigan State University. One day, the chairman of the surgery department called to congratulate me. "You're one of only six applicants we've accepted out of 1,200," he said. "Often, students with straight As don't make the best physicians. But you're a special case. We know you faced a problem, overcame it, and have excelled ever since."

When I reflect on this journey in life, I see any number of events where I could have taken an alternate course. Fortunately, through the encouragement and support of my friends and family, I kept an open mind, listened to myself and those around me who knew best, and chose the path of greatest opportunity.

I meet people from all walks who are not as fortunate, who do not receive the same support and encouragement that I did. People who get stuck in one place and become pigeonholed by the tests they take, or the academic degrees they acquire. Often, these markers only define our future if we choose to let them. Consider that today, nearly three out of every four college graduates work in a field unrelated to their major of study.[1] Many of us, through the guidance of people with good intentions, but who don't truly know, find it difficult to see beyond what a single test or academic pathway tells us.

As Rodger's story illustrates, we need to rely on others to help us see past the artificial limitations we impose on ourselves during our most trying times. These limitations come from a belief that our destiny is determined, a mindset that is not only false but also detrimental to all who embrace it.

---

1 Brad Plumer, "Only 27 percent of college grads have a job related to their major."

I often tell this story as an important business lesson.

The phone rang late one night. I answered it, only to hear the voice of Darryl Berger, a renowned developer in New Orleans who owned and operated the Berger Company.

"Remember what you said about opportunities? Well, I just found one," he said.

I recalled the remark I made to Darryl several months before, just after Hurricane Katrina ravaged New Orleans. I had said to Darryl, "If we believe in the city and in the people here, there are going to be some opportunities." I saw Katrina as devastating but also as a chance to renew and refresh the city, like when the great fires struck San Francisco in the 1930s. I thought I could look at the disaster with either a glass-half-empty or a glass-half-full mindset, and I chose the latter.

"I'm listening," I said.

"It's the Windsor Court Hotel. The Orient-Express is selling it. I think they believe our city is finished."

I pictured the iconic hotel, which had suffered damage from the hurricane but stood as one of the great landmarks of our city that attracted celebrities and people from around the world.

"I'd like you to go in with me on the deal," Darryl continued. "But we need you, Eric."

I listened intently as he spelled out the details. Darryl and two other investors were bidding on the hotel and competing with investors in New York. The others were offering more, but it would take them 180 days to complete their due diligence and close. For Darryl and his partners, and for me if I agreed, it would take 30. As a result, the Orient-Express agreed to award us the bid if we could meet the deadline.

It didn't take much time or consideration to agree. I believed in our city and people. And I trusted Darryl from our time together since Katrina. By coincidence, Darryl and I had each escaped the storm by traveling to Colorado. I stayed with my wife and daughters at a friend's house in Aspen, while Darryl stayed at his house in the nearby town of Snowmass. When I prepared to return to New Orleans, Darryl contacted me. The city would only let people with special clearances reenter, and that included me as a medical director of one of its hospitals. Darryl wanted to view and assess the damage to several real estate properties he owned, and asked if he could return to Louisiana with me. I agreed, and we traveled together only to discover our city transformed. During the trip, we talked about what the city meant to us and how we could help it overcome the disaster.

"Absolutely," I told Darryl on the phone, agreeing to his proposal on the Windsor Court Hotel.

The next day, I met Darryl and two investors. They seemed competent and enthusiastic about the deal, but I discovered that Darryl hardly knew them. One of the investors was a hedge fund manager, while the other owned a shipyard. Still, Darryl seemed confident in them, so I didn't worry. We talked over the details of our operating agreement, which clearly stated that Darryl would assume majority control over the hotel, including its day-to-day operations. Given Darryl's significant experience in hospitality and real estate, everyone agreed with it.

The 30-day deadline was fast approaching. Before I knew it, we reached the eve of the big day.

Then I got another phone call.

"We have a problem," said the voice on the line. It was Darryl, but he didn't sound like his usual self.

"What?"

"They're strong-arming me," he said.

He didn't need to mention our partners. I knew who he meant by "they."

"If I don't give up control, they're out and the deal falls through."

The investors waited until the night before the deadline to request major revisions to the operating agreement. They must have thought Darryl couldn't make the deal without them, and that he would rather change the agreement than lose the deal entirely. If we didn't get the deal done by the next day, it would revert to the investors in New York.

"I don't know what to do," Darryl continued. "Would you be willing to take a higher share?"

In our original arrangement, I would own 25 percent of the hotel.

"I believe in you, and I believe in the city," I said. "And I think what they're doing to you isn't fair. I would like to take their shares. But I don't know about liquidity, if I can get the money to you fast enough so it's all transferred by tomorrow."

"Thank you," he said. "Can we give it a shot?"

When we hung up, I immediately called the bank, which connected me with its president. I explained the situation, the capital needed, and the pressing deadline. I promised to send the loan documents the next day, but I asked for the money to be transferred to my account first.

The bank president didn't say anything at first. It seemed like minutes passed before he talked again. "I'm going to transfer the money because it's you. But if you tell anyone about this . . ."

"Thank you," I said.

I could hardly believe it. From a phone call—no paper, no signature—the money transferred to my account, and Darryl and I became the majority shareholders. We won, while the two investors lost. And soon after, we started renovations on the Windsor Court. Of course, Darryl and I discovered our share of challenges. The investment presented significant risk, and we discovered numerous challenges in restoring the property. Yet it became a great bet, as the hotel soon began making a profit and the New Orleans Saints won the Super Bowl. And our city returned anew, stronger than ever before.

Throughout my life, I have tried to understand the mindset of people like the two investors in this story. A true story from my life. What would cause them to act so callously and foolishly? Why would they see Darryl as an antagonist rather than an ally? I can hypothesize about what fueled their decisions. First, they invariably saw their self-interests as competing with Darryl's, and with my own. For them to win, he needed to lose. Second, the short-term gain of strong-arming Darryl outweighed their long-term relationship with him.

I find many flaws with this thought process. First, their ultimate interests *were* inherently tied to Darryl's and mine, since they needed our investment more than we needed theirs. Second, the short-term return from winning his control was a fraction of the gain from earning his trust. Darryl's extensive knowledge of hotels and vast network of connections would undoubtedly guarantee their long-term success. It just goes to show that the connections we make represent our greatest and most sustainable asset. Business deals come and go, but our partners remain. Why not accelerate our success while helping others do the same?

By protecting their interests over Darryl's, the investors forfeited their best opportunity at acquiring the property. Not only did they lose the asset, but they also forever ended their relationship with Darryl, and gave him fresh motivation to spread the word about their actions to many in the New Orleans business community.

Our connection to others enables us to succeed not only in entrepreneurship but in any arena and capacity of life. Consider my work as a physician. I have built a successful practice, but only through my sincere commitment to helping my patients rediscover normalcy as best I can. Because I wholeheartedly invest my time and energy into my work, I help them, and they return the favor by recommending me to anyone with a hand or upper-extremity issue. In health care, word of mouth represents the best advertising. My practice would not exist today if I saw my patients as transactions or revenue, my colleagues as competitors, and my staff as means to an end. Each stakeholder brings incredible value to the collective, and we all benefit by striving to help one another succeed.

Each of the stories I shared in this chapter—Jason's, Rodger's, and the two investors'—share similarities and differences, but all point to a mindset of "Me" or the absence of recognizing that our connection to others makes us stronger, more capable, and far better off than doing anything alone. A spirit of absolute independence prevents us from seeing others as our ticket to a better life. A belief in a determined destiny forces us to see our future in static form and ignore the endless opportunities around us. The win-lose mindset constricts life to a game of competition in which someone must win and someone must lose, and in which consequences do not apply to how the game is played.

The mindset of "Me" doesn't help us now or in the long run. But luckily, it remains entirely within our control. We can change it today. But first we must recognize it and commit to a new frame of mind—a frame of mind far more inclusive to the people and opportunities around us.

2

The POWER *of* CONNECTEDNESS

I met Danny Calley at a low point in his life. His visit to the clinic happened to coincide with getting laid off from his job. During our first interaction, Danny expressed the fear and uncertainty he faced as the breadwinner with two daughters in college. He described how his first wife had left him, the banks were foreclosing on his house, and he'd lost weight in recent weeks.

"I'm trying to find anything to support my kids in school," he said. "Do you know of any opportunities? I'd take anything that pays well enough."

I sincerely wanted to help him, knowing firsthand the financial pressures that come with supporting a family. I didn't come from wealth or always know success. So I could empathize with Danny and his predicament. As a father, I also valued his commitment to his daughters. My role as a surgeon put me in contact with people throughout the community, and the nature of my work often meant learning about their professional endeavors. As a result, I discovered opportunities where two patients could help one another achieve mutual goals. I might have met a patient who needed to hire someone skilled in finance, and then encountered an accountant who wanted work after graduating from school or getting laid off from his job.

In Danny's case, I had met a struggling entrepreneur who ran a dry cleaner. Operating in a poor location, the entrepreneur feared his business would likely close in the next six weeks, barring a miracle. Not long after, I read an article that discussed the significant demand for dry-cleaning services in New Orleans.

During that first interaction with Danny, I mentioned a possible solution. "You might want to consider picking up people's dry cleaning. You could offer them the same price as any cleaner," I said.

"How could I offer the same price when I've got to pick them up?" Danny asked.

I mentioned what the entrepreneur revealed during our conversation together. He talked about how the cost of dry cleaning dramatically decreased based on volume. I mentioned to Danny that the business owner would likely give him a discount if Danny could promise to bring him the volume needed to keep costs low.

Danny seemed open to the idea. "Would you give me your dry cleaning?" he asked.

"Of course."

He didn't take much convincing. But then I talked to him about the risks and significant sacrifices needed to run a business. Danny would need to invest his life's savings to buy a van and fund an enterprise with no guarantee of succeeding.

"It's like that metaphor about the difference between a bully and a fighter," I told him. "A bully never loses, but a fighter gets beat up. There is no such thing as an entrepreneur who doesn't fail. Anyone who tells you otherwise isn't a real businessperson."

I didn't want to discourage Danny, but I wanted him to understand the risks associated with starting a business. I talked about all my business failures, the stress and anxiety they caused, and how they each taught me important life lessons I would later apply.

"I need to think about this," he said.

I didn't hear from Danny until the end of the week. He asked if I could coordinate the initial meeting with the business owner. I called the dry cleaner and discussed the opportunity.

"That would be great. That would save my business, Dr. George," the owner said.

I made the initial introductions, and for another week, I didn't hear anything. Then Danny called one night and asked if I could help him establish his first route. I suggested that he use our neighborhood; Kim and I would gladly provide him our dry cleaning.

He thanked me, and sure enough, he stopped by our house the next day.

Over the next year, I spoke with Danny intermittently. He called or texted me during the high points and low points in his business. He often talked about the difficulty of working seven days a week, his lack of sleep, and the pressure of running a business, which weighed on his relationship with his daughters.

During these moments, I shared my experiences with Danny to provide him comfort. For instance, the fear I experienced about taking a chance on myself, establishing a health-care clinic, and needing to make payroll and support employees whose livelihoods depended on my ability to run a business successfully.

Danny experienced many challenges, and he called me several times, wondering if his business would make it. Yet he stayed committed, embraced everyone he encountered, and took good care of his people. And over time, his business steadily grew.

Today, Danny operates a very successful business. He owns a dry cleaner and runs a fleet of 40 vans that travel across the city to perform a service that many people need and appreciate, including me. He often jokes that I remain the only nonpaying customer on any of his routes. It pleases me to think about his success since that downtrodden day in the clinic.

When I consider Danny's accomplishments as an entrepreneur, I see them beginning with his hunger to connect with anyone and anything to support his kids going to school. He could have stuck with what he knew and searched for jobs like the one he lost. But he didn't. He embraced the prospect of perhaps needing to find and learn a new career and stayed open to every opportunity. He even jumped at my first suggestion and started a business—betting on himself and an industry he didn't know, which presented far more risk than it did reward. And even as he started to become successful, Danny continued to engage in a mindset of connectedness and, by doing so, built a thriving business.

Danny's story, and indeed the other real-life examples in this book, speaks to the power of connectedness to transform our lives and those around us. Connectedness represents a lifestyle and mindset that drives how we interact with people, ideas, and perspectives on a physical, emotional, social, and psychological level. Connectedness refers to a state of living, not an event or passive activity. Either we are connected or we are not, and this can change at any moment. There also exist varying degrees of connectedness. In this book and in my life, I focus on the highest level of connectedness, nothing less than an unwavering commitment to embracing all manner of people, ideas, and perspectives. A mindset that welcomes a wide slice of life.

My belief in the power of connectedness comes from my work with the hand and, by extension, my significant involvement in the personal and professional lives of the patients for whom I care. The necessity of my work leads to a special bond, a connection in which I help restore an essential part of how my patients live. And through this restoration process, I truly get to learn about how they perceive and experience their world. I gain an unadulterated view into their lives, and while it lasts for the few brief minutes we spend together in the exam room, the hand accelerates the process so I understand them far better than I would in any other context.

In the previous chapter, we explored the problems created by a spirit of absolute independence, a belief in a determined destiny, and a win-lose mindset. Connectedness overcomes each of these lifestyles and points of view. For one, it enables us to recognize that the people we meet, the ideas we encounter, and the perspectives we consider give us strength, and collectively represent our greatest resource for creating the life we want for ourselves and others. It also helps us see that limitless opportunities surround us and the key to unlocking them hides in every new interaction we incite and connection we make. Last, connectedness enables us to build the lasting relationships necessary for mutual gain, relationships that take time to cultivate but provide long-term, sustainable value for all. We can avoid the problems that come from independence, close-mindedness, and a destructive mindset through our connection to others.

Connectedness doesn't simply refer to the connections we make by embracing people, ideas, and perspectives. It also means the way in which we act as intermediaries to connect those who otherwise would never meet or know one another. Danny and the dry cleaner serve as a good example. Danny didn't know the dry cleaner and would likely never have met him, and vice versa. Yet I knew both men and their respective needs, and by staying connected to them, I saw an opportunity to link them in a way that would create value. Not just for Danny and the dry cleaner but also for many others. Danny would benefit by starting his own business, the dry cleaner would profit from saving his, and a great number of people, including me, would see value from receiving a convenient service. And consider the downstream impact. Danny would go on to build a thriving business that would hire many in New Orleans, while the dry cleaner would employ others as well. So many potential connections, such as this one, exist all around us but have yet to form. Connectedness provides us the ability not only to establish our own connections but also to help facilitate them on behalf of other people, which only benefits us as a community, a city, a society, and an economy. The more connected we become, the more we can help others connect. In this way, it becomes an infectious force.

This story also illustrates the importance of selflessness to becoming more connected with those around us. I didn't connect Danny and the dry cleaner to profit from their relationship, but to genuinely help them form a connection that would lead to their mutual gain. Too often, I see the opposite occur. People seek only to form connections that benefit themselves while embracing a mindset of "Me."

Connectedness means looking beyond the self and requires us to focus on others and consider how our connections can benefit everyone around us.

This form of connectedness, bringing separate parties together, doesn't just refer to introducing strangers. It also refers to forming connections between parties who know each other but hold contradictory points of view. These are people who, for whatever reason, cannot consider, or simply refuse to understand, the beliefs of others who don't see the world the way they do.

My work in the clinic serves as a good example. Today, I often find myself working as an intermediary between two traditionally opposed parties: hospital administrators and physicians. Both groups often take conflicting stances on how a hospital should run and how care should be provided. Administrators, on the one hand, focus on the bottom line—the revenue the hospital can generate and the costs it can control. Physicians, on the other hand, focus on patients—their health and the treatments that would improve it. Each focus carries importance, but focusing on one and ignoring the other ultimately hurts everyone, including the patient. A bottom-line-only focus overlooks the crucial services and treatments necessary for optimal care. A patient-only view ignores the financial implications of treatment decisions, which may threaten the viability of the hospital. Both considerations play an important role in the greater system of caring for patients, yet rarely do these groups appreciate them together. As a result, administrators often underestimate the importance of physicians, and vice versa.

Consider my experiences at East Jefferson General Hospital. When I first started working there, the hospital struggled to make money due to inadequate volume. Much of this came from the hospital's inability to perform surgeries efficiently. It performed all types, from the most complex cases to the most routine. For instance, a simple hand surgery would follow a complex coronary bypass, and while the hand procedure would take 30 minutes, the bypass would take hours, often run over time, and cause all subsequent surgeries to get bumped on the schedule. This would mean that the patient going in for a quick procedure would often end up spending the entire day in preop.

Suffice it to say, patients expressed frustration, and so did physicians. Physicians often complained to administrators, and administrators often ignored their concerns, or responded with complaints of their own. As a result, talented practitioners began leaving for hospitals that would give them a voice, and the patient experience further suffered.

I could relate to both sides. I recognized as a practitioner that patients needed a far better experience. I recognized as an entrepreneur that the hospital needed to make money to provide services to begin with. So I approached each group to reconcile their differences. To physicians, I acknowledged their concerns but also presented the other side. To hospital administrators, I addressed their pain points but also introduced the physicians' point of view.

I presented a solution to hospital administrators, and then to physicians. Establish a free-standing ambulatory surgery center that could take the simpler cases, perform them more efficiently, and eliminate all the overhead. Patient volume would increase, wait times would drop, patient experiences would improve, and both administrators and physicians would achieve their desired outcomes. Yet, for it to work according to plan, physicians needed more power and voice in how the center provided services. On their part, physicians needed to embrace the business side of medicine—a side that says you can't perform treatments that exceed the amounts reimbursed for services—and adopt behaviors that improved the bottom line while maintaining the quality of care.

In front of the hospital administrators, I stood at the head of the boardroom and said, "Look. Physicians are your race-horses. They are making you money. You need them just like they need you."

I traversed the halls of the hospital and found physicians in various rooms and break areas. I said to each, "We can't help our patients if we can't keep the doors open. Caring for our patients means also caring for the hospital as a business. We need to balance both, and we can."

To my surprise, the hospital administrators and physicians both listened to me. Not only because I understood their worlds and could articulate them, but also because they each saw me as a member of their exclusive community. Administrators took notice of my success as an entrepreneur and listened. Physicians recognized my experience and talents in performing medicine and paid attention. Yet my success as both a physician and an entrepreneur comes from my ability to connect with the world around me to create value that otherwise wouldn't exist.

We established one of the first freestanding ambulatory centers in the state. Sure enough, all parties benefitted, and they continue to do so. Today, the center stands as a true partnership between the hospital and physicians, with each group sharing equally in its ownership. We still run into differences, but unlike before, the two groups have let go of the win-lose mindset that was holding them back and now pay consideration to each other's points of view. This represents just one of many scenarios where two parties, by overcoming their differences and working together, create significant value for themselves and others. It also shows that when two parties simply cannot come together on their own, it takes a person who embraces connectedness to come between them, foster a dialogue, and facilitate their coordination.

Through my personal experiences and from the many people I encounter in medicine and business, I truly believe connectedness serves as the vehicle to living a life of abundance. It leads to success in all facets, whether professional or personal. A promotion, growth of a business, financial gain. Improved relationships, intrinsic rewards. Connectedness enables everyone to achieve success however they define it, because when we embrace this powerful mindset, we discover the opportunities that reflect our talents, interests, and pursuits, opportunities that enable us not only to feel fulfilled but also to give back to others and contribute in a constructive way.

In the chapters ahead, we explore the possibilities of connectedness by examining six fundamental outcomes. These outcomes interrelate to create a positive self-reinforcing system that supports a rewarding life.

- Outcome #1: Purpose
- Outcome #2: Partnerships
- Outcome #3: Perseverance
- Outcome #4: Support
- Outcome #5: Perspective
- Outcome #6: Trust

We explore outcomes for an important reason. No single path exists to embracing a mindset of connectedness. I don't try to detail a specific step-by-step formula or prescription, because one simply doesn't exist. We all must discover our own paths, because each is unique and depends on our personality, our profession, and the many circumstances that influence our interactions with people, ideas, and perspectives, all of which go beyond the scope of our time together. My purpose in writing this book is to make a compelling case for the importance of connectedness and uncover what we can achieve, and help others accomplish, by adopting this frame of mind.

3

PURPOSE *through* CONNECTEDNESS

After a busy day at the clinic, I sat in my study to catch up on email and saw a message from the editorial staff of *New Orleans Magazine* with the subject line "Congratulations on Selection to the Best Docs List." I opened it and read through the details only to feel pleasantly surprised. The Best Docs List represented the largest annual peer-to-peer survey of those in the medical profession, who selected the top 4 percent of doctors in the country. *New Orleans Magazine* used the survey to further identify the top physicians local to New Orleans and published them in a list by specialty. I felt honored to get that year's distinction, especially since it meant my colleagues would choose me to operate on their hands or the hands of their loved ones. Yet I found my proudest medical achievement in the smaller moments. The artist who couldn't paint but, after a simple procedure, could go on to create masterpieces. The professional football player who couldn't catch a football but could now begin the second phase of his career with a renewed spirit. Or the accountant who couldn't type on a computer but could now resume a career she found rewarding.

It took me years to discover that I wanted to become a hand surgeon. After graduating medical school from Marshall University, I applied for several residencies and got accepted to the Michigan State University for general trauma surgery. I found it deeply rewarding, and it taught me to value family as life's most important gift. While I enjoyed the challenge of general trauma, I sought something different that I couldn't quite identify but could recognize in how I felt. That's when I applied to a fellowship in plastic and reconstructive surgery at Grand Rapids Area Medical Education Center in Michigan. Again, it became another positive learning experience, and I encountered a wide spectrum of injuries. I became most interested in the reconstructive side, where I took care of devastating injuries, including burns. It challenged me in a way far different than plastic surgery, where I treated patients in a drastically different context and from very affluent backgrounds. My work exposed me to patients with high expectations, who demanded perfection, of themselves and especially me, which I found difficult to handle.

Still, something inside me wanted to do something that reflected my passion for meeting and caring for people. That's when I applied to my second fellowship in orthopedic hand

and upper-extremity reconstruction at the Integrated Mayo Clinic in Phoenix, Arizona. Kim made me promise it would be my final fellowship. "You need to get a job," she told me. The two of us had been married several years by then, and I agreed.

Thankfully, hand surgery brought together all the pieces I needed to feel fulfilled while helping my patients overcome devastating injuries, and for many to restore their purpose in life. It exposed me to people from all walks and allowed me to help them in ways that carried great significance to their physical, emotional, psychological, social, and professional well-being. It also provided all the challenges I enjoyed from general trauma surgery. Challenges that come from dealing with the nerve, tendon, and bone. And unlike trauma surgery, or anything else I experienced, hand surgery allowed me to see a high volume of patients quickly.

This brings me to one of the most important outcomes of connectedness: purpose, or discovering how and where to channel our passions, interests, and talents to create shared value that we and others find meaningful. By embracing a wide breadth of diverse people, ideas, and perspectives, we become exposed to many avenues in life, which ultimately help us find where we can succeed and help others do the same. Ultimately, connectedness allows us to discover our purpose by making us keep our eyes, minds, and hearts open, and connecting us with people who know what we don't and can help us along the way. For me, my discovery of hand surgery called for seeking out opportunities, keeping an open mind, and leveraging the advice and experience of my professors and mentors.

Finding our purpose takes a long, circuitous, and sometimes arduous journey. I sincerely believe it takes many years, experiences, and interactions to uncover. I would also say that the journey itself helps create our sense of purpose. Our interaction with others, the knowledge we learn, the wisdom we gain, and the skills we acquire help us find activities where we can create the most value for ourselves and others, and feel fulfilled in the process.

I would also argue that we can live a life of multiple purposes. Surgery represents my purpose in life, yet so does my work as an entrepreneur and investor. All allow me to meet and help people on a micro and macro level. For instance, I can help people individually by operating on their hands, while at the same time, I can scale my reach and impact through the businesses I develop and enterprises I fund. Consider the Pythian. The building carries a rich cultural and historical significance to New Orleans. Tracing its origins back to 1908, it served as one of the first commercial hubs for the African-American community, and it eventually fell into disrepair after Hurricane Katrina. With the help of Barrett Cooper, chief financial officer of ERG Enterprises, we connected with Dr. William Bradshaw, a renowned expert on development. Together, we bought and renovated the Pythian to provide affordable housing to the working class of New Orleans, a segment that previously had been priced out of the market. The project meant tenants could now live and work in the city, and as a result, discover and pursue their passions in life.

"Eric, I want you to take a look at this theater," said Roland on the phone. I stood in one of the empty exam rooms at the clinic, taking a short break between rounds to catch up on calls and emails. Roland called twice that morning on his way to look at properties for sale.

"Which theater?" I asked. "I've only got a couple minutes before my next patient."

"The Orpheum. You really need to see this."

"I'll meet you there after we close," I told him.

Hours later, I left the clinic and drove to meet Roland at the theater. Our history together traced back to a day I operated on his hand. He had cut his thumb welding and nearly severed it completely. For Roland, losing his thumb would essentially mean losing his hand function and, by extension, a hobby and passion he cherished. Fortunately, the procedure saved his thumb, and it established our initial connection.

I approached the Orpheum Theater only to see Roland standing out front. The theater's once-impressive stature looked far less remarkable than the warmly lit Roosevelt Hotel across the street.

"Wait until you check this out," Roland said when I reached him. His smile came into focus as he took me by the shoulder and guided me through the entrance and into the lasting effects of Hurricane Katrina. Even years after the storm, the walls and floors still showed damage from the flooding. The theater existed in a state of disrepair, and a musty smell permeated the interior and only subsided after Roland and I stayed long enough for our senses to acclimate.

We spent another hour touring the theater before leaving. Despite the damage, we saw potential in the lifeless theater and imagined it energized with people and music, the essence of New Orleans. We talked over the details, how Roland knew the broker, how I could put up the capital and Roland could act as the project's developer. I was cautious since Roland seemed personally and emotionally invested in the project, which presented risks to me as his partner. Early on in my career as an entrepreneur, I learned of the danger in falling in love with a project. I could care about and want it, but I needed the capability to realize when it wasn't doing well and make difficult decisions, including getting rid of it.

Still, I saw tremendous upside in the project. At the time, the city was offering tax credits to developers. The project would allow us to capitalize on three different tax credits: one for renovating a historic structure in New Orleans, another for completing a project that promoted the arts, and a third for completing a project supporting music. All said, it would reduce our exposure significantly. As a result, we bought the theater and began planning the renovations.

Meanwhile, I began learning of the immense importance

of this iconic structure to the community. It served as a common point of connection with nearly all my patients, who, after reading daily about the project in the newspaper or watching the news updates each night on TV, eagerly shared their stories with me. Stories from their past, cherished memories they experienced with their parents, spouses, or children. A first date between a couple who would become husband and wife. A routine outing between a son and father, now deceased. A first jazz concert between a mother and daughter, now an aspiring musician. People of all ages, all generations, all walks of life. In every way, the Orpheum brought me closer to my patients and provided a new window into their lives. We shared a connection to the past, present, and future. Their memories, my updates on the plans for the renovations, and our visions for the Orpheum's next iteration.

The banks competed to fund the renovations, and the newspapers and local media continued their daily coverage.

Roland and I talked frequently on the phone.

"Can you believe this? I had no idea this meant so much to everyone," I said. "Did you know?"

"I knew it was important, but I didn't know it was *this* important. No," he responded.

"It's the crown jewel of the city," I continued.

Each of us felt tremendous pressure not only to complete the renovations on time but also to ensure we preserved the rich heritage of the original Orpheum. The theater was constructed in 1918, transformed from a vaudeville theater to a movie palace in the mid-century, nearly demolished in the late 1970s and sub-sequently included on the National Register of Historic Places, and remained as one of the last structures in the country with a vertical hall design, which provided such clarity of sound that audiences could hear a whisper on stage from the balcony. We found photographs of the interior and exterior and used them to guide our renovations and capture the ornate aesthetics. We focused on every detail, down to the black-and-white-checkered feel of the bathrooms. We even went so far as to create our own gold paint for the wall and ceiling designs after discovering that no one manufactured it. Yet we also focused on enhancing the experience with modern innovations. Touch-free faucets, ice machines, a full kitchen, catering, a speakeasy bar.

The renovations continued progressing successfully, on time and according to expectations. As we neared completion, Roland and I targeted August 27, 2015, as the grand reopening of the theater, a date that fell on the 10-year commemoration of Hurricane Katrina.

When we reached the big day, the turnout surpassed our expectations—not only in the volume of attendees but also in the number of recognizable faces. Famous musicians from New Orleans and beyond. Celebrities. Politicians. Athletes. The mayor of New Orleans, the governor of Louisiana, players of the New Orleans Saints. All the pillars of the community visited the Orpheum to relaunch the iconic structure.

One month later, the Louisiana Philharmonic Orchestra (LPO), which for many years called the Orpheum home, returned for the first time since Katrina to celebrate its twenty-fifth anniversary.

Roland and I shared in the city's excitement in getting back its crown jewel. We learned that by reopening the Orpheum, we were helping heal a still-recovering community by restoring a part of it many thought lost forever.

When I reflect on what it took to bring the Orpheum back to life, I see connectedness as a central force. For one, it established my initial connection to Roland that Saturday we met in the clinic. It enabled me to learn about him, hear about his work as an entrepreneur and developer, and help him recover his hand function. It also led to his phone call and request to meet him at the theater. And connectedness also helped us learn from the community and what it valued about the original Orpheum. These lessons proved invaluable to us and guided how we approached the renovations.

This experience taught me that purpose, as it relates to connectedness, refers not only to our life's purpose but also to the meaningful activities, however temporary, that create value for all participants in the equation. The Orpheum today represents this kind of purpose to me. I am now full owner of the theater after buying out Roland, who, as I discovered, was engaged in questionable business activities. Now I see my role as caretaker of this iconic structure, and however long it may last, it represents just one outlet where I can reach people and impact their lives positively.

A young, broad-shouldered man approached me while I was visiting my daughter Chloe at Harvard. He introduced himself as Chuck Katis, a friend of Chloe's, a member of the Harvard swim team and an aspiring entrepreneur.

"Glad to meet you, Chuck," I said.

"You're very successful," he said. "I admire what you've accomplished."

He mentioned what he'd learned about me after becoming friends with Chloe. He talked about my work at Omega, the Hand Center of Louisiana, and half a dozen businesses connected to ERG Enterprises. He immediately impressed me with his intelligence and fascination in developing businesses that could help others.

"When did you meet your friend Chuck?" I asked Chloe after that initial encounter.

She filled me in on how they met and on Chuck's background. He came to Harvard on a swimming scholarship and constantly feared he wouldn't be able to afford tuition. He shared his ideas with Chloe, about the businesses he wanted to start, yet she sensed that he needed encouragement and someone to believe in him.

"Do you have his number? I'd like to call him and see how I can help," I said to Chloe.

Later that week, before making the trip home, I found myself talking with Chuck over coffee. On my part, I imparted the important lessons I'd learned as an entrepreneur, and on his, he discussed his desire to build something remarkable that would help people and improve the conditions of our world. But he mentioned that he didn't know how, and that he wanted to learn from me. To his credit, Chuck was entirely capable of starting his own business. I saw in him a young man with incredible intelligence, good ideas, and enough self-discipline to wake up at 4:00 a.m. every morning to swim. Chuck genuinely wanted to help people and had already demonstrated that he could become an entrepreneur. In high school, he started a nonprofit that visited hospitals and held magic shows for the patients.

"I started Magic of Miracles to help patients see past their illnesses or injuries long enough to get better. I thought if I could accelerate the healing process, if I could make life just a little bit better for them, then that would be worthwhile," he said.

We also talked about his achievements as an athlete, how he broke Harvard's records for the 100- and 200-meter breaststroke, and how he wanted to compete in the Olympics.

I immediately liked and wanted to help him. He struck me as a generous, driven, passionate young man. I decided I would help mentor and father him.

"Let me give you a piece of advice," I said. "*Believe in yourself.*"

Chuck listened intently.

"It doesn't take God-given talent to run a business. You don't need the genetic good fortune of, say, a quarterback in the NFL. Anyone can start a business with a good idea, perspiration, and commitment. I know you possess the capability to manage all three."

Chuck absorbed my words and leaned back in his seat.

"Chloe says you're struggling with tuition?" I asked.

"Harvard's expensive," he said.

Chuck wouldn't tell me he needed money. Finally, I offered him a loan, and only through my insistence did he accept.

"Now," I said. "Chloe says you have a great idea for a business. Tell me about it."

Chuck's shoulders perked up, and his eyes widened. He began talking with more energy. "It's called Mentagrate. It's an app that allows students to find tutors based on what they really need. It's so hard finding a good tutor who can help you. Believe me, as an athlete who needs one, the process is way too difficult, awkward, and ineffective. Plus, it's expensive."

"That sounds like a good idea," I told him. I admitted that I didn't know much about software companies but that several of the people who worked for me at ERG did.

We talked for hours over the details, including his business plan and working prototype.

"Chuck, I want to fund it. I trust and believe in you. And I'd like to help support your mission."

After that day, Chuck and I stayed in frequent communication. I gave him advice and coached him regularly. He, like many young, aspiring entrepreneurs, didn't realize the amount of resources available to him as he sought to build his business. Take angel investors, for instance, many of whom are successful entrepreneurs looking to impart their wisdom and experience on a younger generation with the same desire and hunger to build something remarkable. Or entrepreneurial communities pooling their talents, creativity, and resources to help one another succeed in a world where risk often prevails over reward.

Mentagrate became a success to the point several colleges bought it. But not without perspiration along the way. Chuck encountered great adversity, but true to his nature, he embraced and overcame it. He earned enough capital to fund his next venture, called BodBot, a personal fitness app that helps people plan their workout regimens and manage their diets.

Today, Chuck continues to follow his purpose of helping others through his businesses. And he remains diligent about paying me back. Every month, I receive a check in the mail and a note that thanks me for believing in him.

My connection with Chuck taught me that we can help others discover their purpose in life by extension of ours. My passion and work as an entrepreneur enabled me to coach and support Chuck on his journey, and he hopes to do the same for other aspiring entrepreneurs in the future.

Purpose remains an elusive, yet desirable, goal. From an early age, we begin our quest for discovering what brings us meaning and fulfillment in life. And this journey continues from our childhood years into young adulthood and beyond. In my experience, this journey is necessary and important to finding where we can truly create the most value for ourselves and for others. Yet by embracing a mindset of connectedness, we can at the very least accelerate and improve the process. Rather than passively wait for our purpose to emerge, we uncover the opportunities that lay hidden in the potential connections surrounding us. We can also enlist others to help us find the path that best reflects our talents, pursuits, and interests. Ultimately, connectedness leads to purpose, which reinforces our desire to connect, which fuels a life of abundance. In this way, it becomes a self-reinforcing system, one that unlocks untold value for all involved, value that would otherwise cease to exist.

4

PARTNERSHIPS *through* CONNECTEDNESS

I met A.T. Green during one of his visits to the clinic. He sat across from me in the exam room and talked about his work as a geologist for the oil and gas companies in the 1950s. His work focused on discovering proven and undeveloped fields, or PUDs, across Louisiana. These areas delineated land often rich in oil and worth drilling a well. To encourage geologists like A.T. to discover more PUDs, the oil and gas companies offered an incentive that equates to 5 percent of the oil extracted from each one discovered. The companies saw the offer as favorable, given the modest price of oil and the expected production of the average well.

A.T., using his keen ability to assess land formations and the production of nearby wells, discovered numerous PUDs across the brackish waters of Lafourche Parish to the Texas border.

Over time, the price of oil increased, and the wells pumped out thousands upon thousands of barrels more than initially expected.

The oil and gas industry prospered, and so did geologists like A.T., who saw their monthly dividend payments grow to total millions of dollars.

"That's so interesting," I said to him.

"It's a tale of two different industries," he said. "The funny thing is that the oil and gas companies, when they weren't making much from the wells, they would abandon them."

"Why?" I asked.

"It's kind of like when you drink out of a straw. It's easy when the glass is full, but when it gets close to the bottom, it becomes difficult. You have to suck harder and harder for less and less. Well, the same applies when extracting oil from a well. It gets harder and harder. You pull up sludge. When the price of oil was low, the return didn't justify the operation. So they abandoned them," he said.

"How much oil was left?" I asked.

"Depends. Twenty to thirty percent."

"Wow. The price isn't low anymore."

"Exactly. That's why I retired and started my own exploratory oil and gas company."

Over the weeks and months that followed his surgery, I saw A.T. for his follow-up visits. He talked to me about his hand and recovery, as well as his latest endeavors with his oil and gas venture. Meanwhile, I talked to him about the stories I heard from patients in the oil and gas business, stories that he could relate to and that often made him nod, cringe, or laugh. Our relationship developed to the point we asked about one another's family by first name. I told him about Kim, Chloe, and Cassidy, and the latest adventures in our household.

A year passed, and despite not seeing one another at the clinic, A.T. and I stayed in touch.

Then, one day, a nurse told me a man needed to see me. I entered the lobby only to see A.T.

"How's it going, A.T.? Is everything all right? You're not scheduled," I said.

"I wanted to ask you in person. You know my business?" he asked.

"Of course."

"Well, I wanted to ask if you would be willing to work with me. Look, I know where a lot of these abandoned wells are. I'd like to see if we can bring back what's already there and maybe drill a few more. I know you're fascinated by oil and gas, and I could use a partner."

"I appreciate the offer," I said, surprised. We stood silently in the lobby for a few moments. "I need some time to think about it, I know you understand."

"Take your time," he said. "But it would be great to have you."

That night, I talked it over with Kim. At that point in my early career as a physician, our savings was modest, and I had learned the risks of investing in a business with which I had no expertise. Yet I had also learned the value of finding a partner who brought that expertise and whom I could trust. We talked about the major investment needed, and the risks and rewards of agreeing to the deal. Together, we decided to accept his offer.

The next day, I called A.T. "I'd like to go into business with you," I said.

"Really?" he asked. "I wasn't sure you'd say yes."

"Absolutely. I believe in the business and you as a partner."

Within a year, the partnership proved successful. A.T. demonstrated his gift for tracking down abandoned wells as well as discovering a few PUDs worth drilling. We even named one of the wells "Chlo-Cass" after my daughters. I put most of the revenue in a 529 plan to fund their colleges. It didn't take more than a year for it to pay for their tuition, as the price of oil steadily increased.

A.T. thanked me for partnering with him.

"No," I said. "Thank you."

Connectedness leads to a second outcome: partnerships, or lasting relationships, loyalty, and sources for new ideas, perspectives, and opportunities. Embracing this mindset helps us find and cultivate truly rewarding and sustainable partnerships from our sincere commitment to learning about, investing in, and serving the interests of others.

In my experience, I find that partnerships most often come from discovering our purpose, the first outcome of connectedness, which we explored in the previous chapter. I sincerely believe that when we embrace our purpose in life, strive to help others, and seek to orient our life around people and not ourselves, we naturally cultivate the partnerships that produce the most value for all involved. For instance, when I met A.T. on our first encounter, I focused on how I could channel my purpose of hand surgery to help heal his ailment. Yet I often encounter the opposite mindset in business. A mindset where people focus solely on how they can profit from a deal, with no consideration paid to the person on the other side of the table. They take a "What's in it for me?" approach to every interaction. Or they expect something in return for any effort they put forth.

The most successful people I encounter in life and business embrace a far different mindset. They see relationships as the strongest and most sustainable asset, and people as the means and the end to value creation, rather than just the means. Consider our work at ERG Enterprises, for example. As a philosophy, we invest in partners first and projects second. We believe a good partner can make up for a bad project, but a good project can never make up for a bad partner. This philosophy has enabled us to acquire and operate many of New Orleans's most iconic properties, and it has also led to investments in remarkable businesses across multiple industries. By embracing connectedness, we have successfully found partners who share our passion and vision. In real estate, this means finding people who seek to invest in projects that do not just produce a profit but also create value for people and our planet (what we call "the triple Ps").

My partnership with A.T. enriched both our lives. For one, it introduced me to a man I genuinely liked and whose stories of oil and gas expanded my knowledge of the industry, stoked my curiosity, and generated a variety of emotions, all of which improved my day. It also introduced me to a wonderful business opportunity that would pay for my daughters' education, produce other connections in oil and gas, and provide the capital for future business deals.

My role as a care provider naturally lends itself to these partnerships. Invariably, patients see in me a trusted advisor and ally in the war they wage against their injury or illness. Still, I find my greatest partnerships start with my genuine interest in learning about people, my curiosity about their lives, and my ongoing commitment to unearthing the experiences and knowledge that make them unique. This is to say, you don't need to become a physician to establish truly lasting partnerships. I believe we can all benefit from engaging in a more person-oriented, accommodating approach no matter what profession we hold or what context we find ourselves in. We can all profit by seeking to learn where our interests intersect with others and our backgrounds overlap, as well as where they don't. Once we embrace this mindset, we become far more capable in developing sustainable and rewarding partnerships.

Partnerships exist in many forms, none more important than family. The role our families play in our lives calls for a deeper level of connectedness, and only increases the need for us to stay open-minded, attentive, and curious about their ideas and perspectives, even when they differ from our own. In every way, family serves as the core, and its strength either enhances or hinders our ability to form partnerships outside of it. My partnership with Kim, Chloe, and Cassidy continues to enrich my life, strengthens my resolve, and adds meaning and fulfillment to what would otherwise lack it. The same is true for my father, mother, and brothers.

I recall one summer when we wanted to take a family trip to Africa.

"Dad, I don't just want to go to Africa," Chloe said. We sat at the dining room table, discussing our upcoming family trip. "I don't just want to be a tourist. I want our visit to matter."

Cassidy agreed with her older sister.

Kim and I looked at each other and smiled.

"Okay, well, tell us what we should do, then," I said.

Several days passed before Chloe and Cassidy introduced their plan. Again, we sat together for dinner.

"There's an orphanage in Kenya," Chloe said. "It's a charity school that was built last year and serves underprivileged children."

"Where in Kenya?" Kim asked.

"Mombasa," Cassidy said.

"Look, we'll show you." Chloe left the room only to return with her laptop. The four of us huddled around it and looked at the pictures of people visiting a small wooden hut in rural Africa. Underneath the picture, a caption mentioned how the school served 160 students, mostly orphans.

"Is it safe?" Kim continued.

"Of course." Chloe clicked on the website and pulled up pictures of other families making the trek.

"This would make for a memorable trip," Chloe continued.

Weeks later, we traveled to Mtongwe, one of the poorest suburbs in Mombasa. When we arrived at the Destiny Garden School, we saw the small wooden hut from the picture as well as a few buildings under construction. Thankfully, Chloe and Cassidy suggested we bring medical and educational supplies before we made the trip. Several teachers thanked us upon our arrival and talked about their significant need for the basic provisions.

We started building a new nursery for the school. It took a couple weeks to finish construction, and on the day of its completion, Chloe and Cassidy cut a red ribbon to commemorate its opening.

And then something surprised us. We thought the schoolchildren would race into the building and express awe at the additional space afforded to them. Sure enough, they did, only to lie down one by one on the concrete floor. We stood outside the entrance, watching the students as they lay motionless, their bare chests planted on the hard surface.

"They've never seen concrete before," one of the teachers told us when we asked what their reactions meant. "All they know is dirt. And the concrete is cool on their bodies."

We made the trip back to New Orleans, where we discovered a new perspective and appreciation for our life and everything afforded to us. We began to perceive just how much we take for granted. A cement-paved street, a lobby filled with air conditioning, access to education, resources for basic medical care, and so on. Chloe's recommendation made our family trip one none of us will ever forget. And it symbolizes the power of family to enrich our lives, which truly enables us to accomplish the goals and aspirations we set for ourselves and our loved ones.

"You're a hand doctor," Dallas Snadon said. We'd met Dallas and her husband, Daryl, only a couple hours before. Our friends had invited us to their house in Aspen for dinner, along with the Snadons. It only took the mention of my profession for Dallas to make this last statement.

"Yes, I am," I said.

"I've been unable to ski and I'm an avid skier," Dallas continued. She mentioned how earlier that year, her doctor had diagnosed her with rheumatoid arthritis. At dinner, she described how the crippling pain prevented her from pursuing the activities she enjoyed most in life. "I've seen people from around the country. No one knows what to do."

I asked to examine her hand. She extended it, and everyone around the table grew quiet for a time.

"You need surgery," I said.

She looked surprised. "Really?"

"Yes."

"No one has ever told me that. I've seen, gosh, I don't know how many doctors. Great ones. Nobody has recommended surgery."

I explained my reasoning, how by removing one of her bones and rolling up a tendon, the pain would go away.

"Do you think I could get back to playing tennis and skiing if I did this?" she asked.

"I do," I said.

Daryl stood from the table. "If you can get my wife skiing again, you would change all of our lives," he said.

Later, after dinner, we arranged for Dallas to undergo surgery in New Orleans. The night ended with Dallas talking about her love for skiing and the first run she would choose if the surgery proved successful.

One week later, Dallas and Daryl flew to New Orleans. They met me at the clinic, and the surgery went according to plan. After they return to Aspen, Daryl and I stayed in touch. Over the following weeks and months, he frequently texted and updated me about Dallas's progress. One day, he sent a picture of Dallas at the foot of a white powdered slope with "THANK YOU" below it.

Then, one night, I received another text from Daryl, this one inviting Kim and me to travel back to Aspen for a week. "We want to show our appreciation," his text read.

Kim and I talked it over, and we agreed to make the trip. We stayed with the Snadons at their home.

We enjoyed the time, and after several days, Daryl presented an opportunity.

"Eric," he said. "You know, I'm getting ready to develop a lot here in Aspen."

I knew of Daryl's success as a developer. He had recently built and sold a 25,000-square-foot house on the sought-after Willoughby Way of Red Mountain for $43 million. The deal set a record at the time and garnered national and regional attention, not just because of the price tag but also because of Daryl's creative use of transferable development rights (TDR) to overcome Aspen's recent restrictions on acquiring land over 6,000 square feet.

The lot he mentioned during the trip equaled 30,000 square feet.

"I don't really need partners," Daryl continued. "But maybe we could do something together. I've always thought about getting a partner, and I'm getting older now. Look, I'm very appreciative of what you did for my wife. Let's partner on this."

We discussed the opportunity in more depth. I saw it as a high-risk deal, something I wouldn't normally pursue. But I liked Daryl and his wife, and I believed in him.

Daryl must have sensed my anxiousness. "At the end of the day, if we build this thing and it doesn't sell, then you'll have 50 percent of the house. And I've already got two houses out here, so I don't need a third one."

I considered the risks and rewards of the deal with an open mind. For one, Daryl did this for a living and built his fortune selling houses all over Aspen for the ultrawealthy. Billionaires knew him by first name and sought him out. And in Aspen, owning a Snadon home carried distinction. As a worst-case scenario, I would end up owning a beautiful house in Aspen that my family and I could use.

"Of course," I said. "I appreciate you bringing me in on this."

The next week, when I returned to New Orleans, I sent him a check for my half of the lot.

We built the house and hand decorated it. And two years later, it sold to a billionaire for double what Daryl and I had invested.

My connection with Daryl taught me several important lessons about the value of partnerships. For one, they truly expand our knowledge of the world around us. My work with Daryl and curiosity in his business taught me about real estate development, which I would later use in other deals. His insights, for instance, informed how I would later approach the reconstruction of the Orpheum Theater, the restoration of the Pythian, the development of the Omni Royal Hotel, and the renovation of the Pontchartrain Hotel.

I also learned that the partnerships we establish through connection reinforce our ability to connect with and establish relationships in the future. In other words, the partnerships we develop today lead to potential connections we can make tomorrow. My experiences with Daryl may help me establish rapport with another developer I encounter. Or it might help me establish a connection with someone who understands the housing market in Aspen, who lives in Colorado, or who simply heard about the town's expensive housing market.

Partnerships extend our personal and professional networks exponentially. They expand our networks to include those of our partners, and vice versa. At ERG Enterprises, for instance, our portfolio of investments continues to fuel its own expansion. One partner refers us to another in his or her network, which leads to another connection in the future, and so on. Today, if I meet someone interested in buying real estate in Aspen, I refer him to Daryl, and if he meets someone needing hand surgery or someone connected in New Orleans, Daryl refers him to me. And depending on the kind of partnership, this network might expand to include connections of connections. For instance, a person I know who knows someone else who might be able to help. And this represents just one partnership. Think about the power and reach when we consider all the partnerships we acquire and maintain over the course of our lives.

My commitment to connectedness means I have cultivated truly lasting and rewarding partnerships, and continue to do so. I find partnerships a prerequisite to living a fulfilling and abundant life. While purpose provides us satisfaction by allowing us to channel our talents, passions, and interests, partnerships enables us to form the bonds that stoke our intellect, expand our perspective, challenge our understanding of the world, and satisfy our desire for social interaction.

Like many lessons explored in this book, there is no one-size-fits-all definition of partnerships. They can take different forms and produce different outcomes, but the most valuable and rewarding kind come from a deep foundation of connectedness. They are by no means limited to business deals either; we can form partnerships in any aspect of our lives to achieve our goals and find our purpose, and to help others do the same. The greatest partnerships of my life, my partnerships with my wife Kim, and my daughters, Chloe and Cassidy, have nothing to do with business and everything to do with forming the deepest, most lasting connection possible. The more connected we become, the stronger our relationships, and the greater the collective value experienced.

5

PERSEVERANCE *through* CONNECTEDNESS

In 2005, I learned a very important lesson in business: success brings as much turmoil as failure. When the business thrives, people sue you just as often and frequently as when it flounders.

I learned about the opportunity to buy Omega Hospital as a physician at East Jefferson General Hospital (EJGH). A professional acquaintance named Dr. Bellini became chronically ill and offered to sell it to me. I made my first mistake in sharing the opportunity with an administrator at EJGH and giving him the first right of refusal. He congratulated me and declined the offer, but asked that I not pirate, or recruit, any of the doctors from East Jefferson. This forced me to look outside the core network of physicians I knew well and trusted. Soon, I assembled a team of 12 talented surgeons who agreed to buy the hospital with me. The deal went through successfully, and I entered the next phase of my life with majority ownership and control of Omega.

One of the physicians was named Najeeb, a young surgeon who demonstrated an insatiable hunger to succeed not only as a surgeon but also as a businessman. Immediately, Najeeb sought my advice in a variety of areas—from running a practice to hiring staff to making investments. His passion and desire to learn made me embrace him as an apprentice. Rather quickly, our relationship developed. Kim and I even helped him find a house in our neighborhood. Najeeb owned only a small percentage of Omega, but I viewed him as one of the more promising physicians at our practice.

Yet that began to change. Over time, I began to hear rumors about Najeeb that I couldn't believe at first. When buying Omega, I managed to recruit a couple physicians I shared a history with and knew I could trust. They began questioning Najeeb's motives. "He's got a lot of time on his hands lately," one of them told me. "And he's spending most of it meeting with the other doctors, telling them they deserve to be making more."

The comment seemed shocking. For one, the government outlawed basing reimbursement on production, given obvious safety risks. And second, after its first year, Omega paid out millions in distributions to the physicians, based on their percentage of ownership.

Despite their commentary, I never witnessed Najeeb's extracurricular activities. My position as president and chief executive officer of Omega, coupled with the fact I still consulted patients and performed surgeries, consumed all my time, energy, and focus. In a relatively short period of time, we revolutionized the hospital's operations, maximizing efficiencies in workflow and enhancing quality of care and the patient experience. And this occurred during a time when reimbursements were high, all of which contributed to a healthy bottom line.

The hospital kept me more than distracted. Then, on a business trip, I received a call from one of my loyal physician partners. He spoke quickly on the phone. "You're not going to believe this," he said.

"What?" I asked.

"I just left a meeting that Najeeb led. He made a PowerPoint that showed how much everyone made last year. He had a graph and everything. Now some of the physicians don't think they're being compensated fairly."

"They're making ten times what they did previously," I said.

Soon after, I received a notice that Najeeb and several physicians had filed a lawsuit. It alleged that I, along with my loyal partners, diverted money from Omega to our personal accounts. The group sued me, my partners, and every company I owned at the time. They also filed a separate tax return to the Internal Revenue Service to trigger an audit of Omega.

To make it worse, they began filing complaints that attacked my character and personal reputation.

The onslaught happened quickly and abruptly. I sought the advice of my father and brother, both practicing attorneys. My father shook his head in anger and could hardly steady his voice. "Son, you need to find an attorney who will not only kill him but drive the sword into his heart and onto the ground," he said.

"You've never been in a lawsuit. This is going to be the most difficult time in your life. It's going to rock everything," my brother Anthony said. "You need to remember to take care of Kim, Chloe, and Cassidy. It's going to be hard on all of you."

He was right. Before the court hearings even began, I could see the stress interject itself into our lives and absorb our attention. Lively conversations at the dinner table soon became quiet, reserved gatherings. A cloud of uncertainty weighed us down.

Still, someone needed to lead Omega, grow the business, and take care of the patients who depended on us. I kept up with my busy schedule, often forcing myself to ignore the ordeal and hustle to keep the hospital intact.

Through this process, I made the fortunate move of hiring Peter Butler, the smartest attorney I'd ever met. Peter knew how to outmaneuver the competition in a courtroom. He immediately recommended I hire a lawyer to represent each company, including Omega. Because I owned controlling interest in the hospital, and because of my role as CEO, I could direct the counsel to act in the best interests of the organization. I told Omega's attorney to stop all distributions since the hospital needed the funds. Effectively, this move diverted millions of dollars from the plaintiffs to defend against their lawsuit. They began footing the entire bill, which became one of the most expensive in Louisiana's history, with dozens of motions filed each day over a period of months. It escalated to a point where the situation appeared unsustainable. Peter called me then and said we should try to settle. "They're obviously hemorrhaging. Let's see if they're willing to buy you out."

"Peter, I don't know if I want to sell," I said.

"Let me ask you a question. Would you want to buy them out?"

"It depends what it would take. Of course I'd like to get rid of them and salvage the asset."

"That's why we're having this meeting. Not so you sell, so they do."

Peter and I discussed the worth of the hospital. We eventually settled on a fair asking price of $18 million. Both of us knew the plaintiffs couldn't afford it.

We held the meeting, presented the figure, and sure enough, they came back with a price far lower than $18 million. Several rounds of negotiations ensued until the physicians eventually set the price at $8 million.

Peter again asked if I wanted to buy Omega. "Of course," I told him. It would represent a substantial investment, one not without substantial risk. Yet I knew its worth far exceeded its cost if my trusted team and I could continue leading it. The banks would loan the capital, which wouldn't take long to pay off if we sustained our growth.

"Dr. George will buy you out for that amount," Peter told the plaintiffs, a brilliant move on his part. He knew they would severely discount the value of the hospital, and once they firmly set a price, they couldn't walk back from it. It left them with two options: settle or continue to bleed money paying for the litigation.

They chose to settle. The seemingly endless war concluded in the courtroom, in a scene that could have come from a movie. The judge looked down from his chair at the plaintiffs. "Gentleman," he said, "you have killed the goose that was laying golden eggs." He was right. They tore off its wings and broke its neck.

I took full ownership of Omega and continued to enhance its emphasis on a quality, luxurious experience for patients and efficiency in care. We installed Murphy beds in every patient room so family members could stay overnight with their loved ones as they recovered. We also added big-screen TVs, mini fridges, and other accoutrements to help patients feel comfortable and ultimately heal faster. We made numerous enhancements down to every minuscule detail. And as a result, it only took a couple months of distributions for the hospital to pay for itself.

I rewarded everyone who had stayed loyal. That included a few physician partners as well as the many employees, housekeepers, groundskeepers, nurses, and staff who didn't want the other group of physicians taking over.

Omega offered me an early glimpse into the vicious nature of business, which inevitably accompanies success and which we can never truly circumvent. It also taught me the immeasurable value of finding people you can trust and rely on. Despite my helping Najeeb, he betrayed my friendship and trust—and it appeared all for money. He taught me that the more successful we become, the more challenges we encounter, and the more necessary it becomes to fight for what we truly value.

When we look at success, whether as a professional athlete or as a businessperson, we tend to overlook the significant sacrifice, hard work, and commitment it takes to reach that position in life. Steve Jobs once said, "Half of what separates the successful entrepreneurs from the non-successful ones is pure perseverance."[1] Thomas Edison said, "Genius is 1 percent inspiration, 99 percent perspiration." Consider some of the most successful people today—for example, Jeff Bezos, or Bill Gates and his partner Paul Allen. To put it simply, they worked tirelessly. They willingly invited risk, stress, and challenges into their lives, knowing the rewards justified them. And they continued to hustle and stay resolute no matter how many times they failed. It takes definite self-confidence, passion, and tolerance for adversity. In the case of Bill Gates and Paul Allen, Allen said they would put a computer in every household in the US. At that time, it seemed an unbelievable proposition, given the size and expense of computers then. The sheer magnitude of their vision brought tension into their personal and professional lives. Rather than back down, they

---

1   Tor Constantino, "Five Leadership Lessons from Steve Jobs," *Michael Hyatt*, November 4, 2011.

wrestled with it, and ultimately became triumphant. Consider innovations widely available today. Imagine at the turn of the century, envisioning a world where smartphones would transform our lives—from how we bank or travel to how we communicate and consume information. Even the most creative minds would become skeptical at the thought. Yet someone envisioned this dream and maintained the courage to pursue it no matter how many obstacles stood in the way.

Success doesn't represent a lottery ticket. It doesn't come from luck but from tireless work and remarkable sacrifice. I didn't wake up one day with the capital I needed to buy Omega. I earned it, only after many years of working seven days a week, taking educated risks, and compiling my wealth. This journey started when I first moved to New Orleans and took emergency room calls because I wanted to build my reputation as a physician. I covered every emergency room in the city, realizing early on that success requires more than just ability, but also affability and availability. I built rapport with important people in the community, and I developed significant insight into how to operate a health-care organization successfully. Everything I learned and accomplished on this journey contributed to my eventual success as an entrepreneur. My work as a physician created the opportunity to own my practice. Health care led to hospitality, which opened the door to real estate, which created opportunities in entertainment, technology, aviation, and so on. One investment created the chance to make another and another. Over time, my opportunities increased, my network expanded, and my knowledge improved, but my underlying commitment to working hard, accepting risk, and embracing challenges remained fundamentally the same.

Through this journey of success, I also experienced plenty of failures. Yet I didn't let them diminish my confidence or slow my momentum. Rather, I saw each experience as a learning opportunity. Omega taught me to fight for what I value. Looking back, I could have easily given up, reverted to working as a physician, and allowed Najeeb and the other surgeons to take over. In many ways, I see this as one of the benefits of connectedness. It truly allows us to recognize the full potential of the opportunities afforded to us and recognize that we can always surmount any obstacle with hard work, the right approach, and access to people who can support us along the way.

In the case of Omega, I also learned greed never helps anyone and it represents the least sustainable behavior. In fact, it signals a losing game for the person who lets it control their mindset and actions. Just ask the plaintiffs in the Omega case, who lost millions because they wanted more and couldn't appreciate what they had acquired.

My experiences also taught me that sometimes the "We" needs to fight for you. It reminds me of something my daughter Chloe said while I was writing this chapter. We talked about Omega and recalled the stress of the experience. Chloe remembered all the sleepless and stressful nights I spent talking to lawyers and fretting over what the next day would bring. "Dad, you're a one-man army," she said. It pleased me to hear her stick up for her father. The entire ordeal required strength and toughness, not just on my part. Truthfully, my success also depended on the remarkable people surrounding and supporting me. Peter Butler, for instance. Or Chloe, Cassidy, and Kim, who provided the essential support I needed just to survive.

We must give people a square count rather than attempt to outmaneuver or outsmart them. Opportunities don't always work out in business or life. The most successful people accept this and understand that ultimately their greatest asset doesn't reside in a property or company, but in their partners. Rather than trample them, they nurture and support them, conduct themselves honestly, and as a result, win far more deals than they lose.

6

SUPPORT *through* CONNECTEDNESS

I first met Barrett Cooper, who would become my chief financial officer at ERG Enterprises, through our mutual connection to Darryl Berger. Barrett called me one day after Darryl gave him my contact information. Barrett's voice sounded friendly and passionate as he talked about his experience in real estate, his education from Vanderbilt and Tulane universities, and his interest in coming to work for me. He had worked, for a time, at a large development firm before choosing to start his own company. He learned very quickly, as most aspiring entrepreneurs do, of the difficulty of running a business, especially one that required him to rely on banks for capital. Barrett found incredible properties that presented tremendous upside, yet he lacked the financing to secure loans from the banks. They simply saw him as too great a risk. After several interactions, I presented him the opportunity to help ERG Enterprises on a few real estate deals. After all, I saw a bright young man hungry to succeed and eager to learn. Very quickly, he demonstrated his intelligence and, quite honestly, his brilliance. He showed a knack for making connections with people in real estate and finding great opportunities for investment, and he demonstrated impressive talent and expertise for evaluating the financial implications of a deal. Barrett brought a passion and vision we all shared at ERG, as well as a lacking piece of talent and experience that could help our enterprise grow. I hired him full-time to bring organization to ERG, manage our existing relationships with partners, and find new opportunities.

I have always understood the importance of relying on others whom I can trust and who bring the intelligence and capability to help me achieve mutual goals. As a surgeon, my time and attention remain concentrated on my patients and the intricate nuances of neurons, tendons, and bones. This means that I must depend on others to make critical decisions on my behalf and trust them to run ERG. Success in any discipline requires depending on others and accepting the reality that we don't know all the answers. Yet we can find them by connecting with others who can add more detail to the picture. I have never met a successful entrepreneur who didn't take a chance on his people, delegate essential responsibilities, and relinquish control. At the same time, I have never met a successful entrepreneur who didn't find the right people to work for him, people who could bring something unique to the enterprise, share in the collective passion and vision of the company, and seek to succeed at no one's expense other than his own hard work. People like Barrett.

This brings me to another outcome of connectedness: support, or developing a team of trustworthy people who share our passion and contribute to our purpose. Support calls for not only hiring talented employees or finding valuable partners but also sustaining and maximizing these relationships for the universal benefit of everyone. It took great care in vetting Barrett as someone who could truly advance our mission as a business, but once he checked out, it became imperative for me to help him excel in his role and achieve his purpose in life. I empowered Barrett to make decisions on my behalf, run the business as he would his own, and take full ownership of managing our portfolio. While we gained his time, talent, and expertise, Barrett gained work he remains passionate about and security he lacked as a struggling entrepreneur. It underscores that the more connected we become, the more we can find the right people to support our mission in life, and the more we can help nurture their goals and needs.

Today, Barrett continues to help ERG grow by managing our portfolio across numerous industries. He also continues to discover some of our greatest investments. The key to Barrett's success comes from his ability to connect with others, recognize opportunities, and stay open-minded. For example, Barrett is wholly unafraid to learn new disciplines, businesses, or industries. He doesn't shy away from people who hold more experience or expertise than he does; rather, he seeks to study them and form new connections with people who can enrich his life professionally, personally, and intellectually.

One of Barrett's most successful projects was the Pythian, a building that brings great historical relevance to the New Orleans African-American community. A wealthy former slave commissioned its construction in 1908, and for a time, it stood as the largest structure owned by an African American in the country. It represented a beacon of economic promise in the black community, as it contained many businesses either owned by or tailored to African Americans. The Pythian also represents the origin of jazz in New Orleans. Its roof featured a jazz hall that brought together famous musicians, including Louis Armstrong. Our involvement in the Pythian came from Barrett's outreach to William Bradshaw, a fellow real estate developer who acquired the property with plans of renovating it. Barrett knew of the Pythian's long history and congratulated William. And as the two talked, Barrett learned that William needed funding for his project, and Barrett quickly offered our assistance.

It proved a fortunate meeting for all parties. The funding William had secured for the renovations fell through when the banks retracted their offer. It left William and his company Green Coast Enterprises with an asset and no capital to fund its reconstruction. Barrett was the first person to encourage that we support William's project. After all, he knew of its worth far better than anyone else. He also knew that it aligned with the three Ps that comprise ERG's investment philosophy:

people, planet, profit. The Pythian would benefit the people of New Orleans by providing affordable housing to the working class, a segment that the real estate market didn't serve. People who fell into this category made too much money annually to qualify for subsidized housing, and they couldn't afford the high-end apartments sprouting across the city. The Pythian would offer workforce-rate apartments to people making 80 to 120 percent of the average median income, which included most people working in New Orleans, many of whom staffed the local hospitals and businesses essential to our city. The project would also protect the planet because it didn't require destroying an existing structure to build something new, but rather, it called for enhancing a dilapidated landmark that already existed. And of course, because every business needs to make money, it would generate profit. To William's credit, he crafted an ingenious plan of using governmental tax credits—offered to incent development after Hurricane Katrina—to acquire and renovate the property relatively inexpensively.

Together, Barrett and I decided that we wouldn't just provide funding to William; we would help him codevelop the Pythian. That meant getting deeply involved with its renovation and operations. As with the Orpheum Theater, we knew of its significance to the New Orleans community and sought to preserve its rich history. To this end, we conducted extensive research and began plans to restore its original design. Most visibly, this included removing the cladding from the building's façade—constructed in the 1950s—and reinstating the beautiful tan brick, terra cotta, and grand stone entrances that adorned the original.

We also sought to create more than living quarters, but also a center for commerce and social activity that would revitalize the neighborhood. My patients who worked in the area often talked about the need for more convenient, diverse, and affordable food options. In response, we developed plans for a 20,000-square-foot food hall that would appeal to a broad range of culinary tastes. And it would also provide much-needed space for social gatherings and events to bring people together. In the area, people also needed affordable, convenient health-care services, a reason we designed space for a health-care and physical therapy clinic.

The Pythian reopened in early 2018 as a beacon of promise in New Orleans. Importantly, the building, and our involvement, continues to bring me closer to my new and existing patients, because it serves as a common point of connection and dialogue. I meet many who live there, work there, or eat at its food hall. They share their excitement, experiences, and the significance of the Pythian to their life or profession. I share in their enthusiasm and tell their stories to Barrett, and in many cases, we learn from their experiences to improve them.

Without Barrett, we wouldn't be involved in the Pythian or several other important investments. Of course, I also owe my success and that of ERG Enterprises to many other partners I trust and rely on—Greg Anderson, for instance, an investment banker I first met when I considered selling Omega

Hospital. Greg and I worked together on a few deals before he pitched the idea of coming to work for me. I saw in Greg, as I do in Barrett, a person with an incredible talent, expertise, and passion for his work that truly aligns with our mission as a business and that enriches my life. He continues to introduce me to remarkable entrepreneurs who expand my knowledge of industry and business, and who willingly embrace my advice and mentorship. Take for example a company that helps school districts adopt new technology and improve student outcomes, or a medical-supply company that provides affordable test strips to diabetes patients to increase self-care and treatment adherence. Importantly, Greg continues to find and present me with opportunities that not only benefit our business but also help solve a problem of great significance to people. For his part, Greg enjoys the freedom and autonomy of working on his own for our collective benefit. And in many ways, his success comes from his ability to connect with others, learn about them personally and professionally, and remain constantly curious. As a result, Greg has built his own reliable team to support his endeavors. Today, he represents someone I greatly depend on.

When it comes to my practice, I rely on numerous people, such as Craig Henry, my office manager. Craig oversees the daily operations at our clinic, and I depend on him to stay attuned to the details to which I can't attend. Of his many responsibilities, he remains essential to hiring talented professionals. He often tells me that hiring new people represents the most challenging responsibility, and I agree. Yet Craig continues to find trustworthy, passionate, open-minded, and talented individuals, characteristics that Craig shares and that I believe make him successful in this regard. I also see his success as the outcome of his ability to connect with others.

Success in life requires great individual accomplishment, yet no achievement comes without the help and support of a team working together. The success of a company does not come as the result of one person's brilliance but from the collective wisdom of people pooling together their time, talents, and expertise. For a surgeon, establishing a successful practice requires assembling a team of reliable and capable nurses, support staff, and professionals in ancillary functions, such as accounting, finance, and billing. The more I invest my time and energy into recruiting people who share my passion for medicine, seek to help patients and accommodate their needs, and stay open-minded and problem-solve, the more patients I can see, the better treatment I can provide, and the more successful our practice can become. Finding the right people is even more paramount considering the number of factors that can influence patient outcomes, and the coordination needed to maximize the number of patients who flow through the facility each day.

When I started my first practice, I found that embracing a mindset of connectedness allowed me to find the first iteration of people who could grow our practice. And because I sought people who also embraced this philosophy, they in turn found the next iteration of talented personnel, who did the same when the time arrived. It enabled our practice to grow, my work to expand beyond medicine into entrepreneurship, and our reach to move into new industries and impact more people in new ways. Today, Craig and the other talented professionals who support my work in the clinic enable me to fulfill my passion of meeting and helping people to recapture an identity they temporarily lost. I depend on them to maximize the people I can reach and impact on any given day. And that means taking care of all the details to which I can't attend—cleaning and disinfecting the rooms; taking histories, X rays, and vitals; checking patients in and out; and so on.

Yet I also depend on my business partners and those who support our mission at ERG Enterprises to improve communities worldwide. I rely on these individuals not only to bring expertise that adds value to our company but also to serve as an extension of my time and capacity so I can practice medicine. At the same time, I rely on these partners to enhance my connections—to introduce me to new people, businesses, industries, and opportunities. In every way, my support team allows me to lead an enriching life. Medicine fulfills my deep desire for human interaction, while business stimulates my curiosity for new ideas, business models, approaches, and perspectives. Yet importantly, I must take care of the people who support me, by empowering them, ensuring they feel fulfilled, and helping them achieve their goals in life. Connectedness, by definition, embodies a mutual exchange.

Truthfully, we never accomplish anything of importance without people helping us along the way. No matter how difficult a surgery or miraculous its outcome, or how smart a business decision, success does not depend on "Me" but on the collective contributions of everyone supporting the organization.

7

PERSPECTIVE *through* CONNECTEDNESS

A woman from a religious mission in New Orleans stopped by the clinic one day. She told me about a nine-year-old boy named Faruk, whom her organization had found begging on the streets of Ethiopia and had managed to rescue and fly to the United States. She described the severe burn injury he had suffered years earlier, when his house burned down, killing his family. The woman asked if I could help Faruk regain his hand function. I told her to bring him by the clinic and I would try my best.

A week later, the tall, frail boy entered the clinic and sat across from me in the exam room. Faruk suffered a burn-scar contracture, which meant the fire burned the skin of his hands to the point it pulled together with the skin of his wrists, resulting in deformity.

Despite the severity of the injury, Faruk appeared upbeat during our first encounter. He smiled as I examined his hands, which made me think he felt grateful to escape the extreme poverty of his life in Africa. Regardless of his attitude, I didn't know if the boy would ever regain his hand function. I remember thinking it would take a miracle for him to ever experience a normal life.

Over the next year, I operated on Faruk half a dozen times until he could freely use his hands. He still faced tremendous obstacles, including the need to undergo three years of exhaustive rehabilitation. Still, through all of this, I never once heard Faruk complain about his condition, the chronic pain he experienced, or the procedures he endured. Rather, he maintained the same smile and personality that characterized him. And upon successful completion of his rehabilitation, Faruk left our care to renew his life.

Approximately 20 years later, he returned to the clinic to say thank you. Unfortunately, I didn't see him. I remember listening with joy as the nurses described the tall, handsome, 30-year-old man who stopped by to see me. He introduced himself as Faruk, the boy from Ethiopia, and told the staff to tell me about his life. Faruk still lived in the United States after traveling back to Ethiopia for a time. He graduated law school and became a practicing attorney, and recently started a family.

Still, I think about Faruk on most days when I encounter a patient with an especially gruesome injury or meet someone who can't envision life after their illness—for instance, a patient who needs to undergo a toe transfer, which requires the removal of a toe to replace a lost or injured finger. It represents just one of many cases that require a remarkable strength of spirit. To these patients, I speak about a boy who faced remarkable odds but successfully overcame them with a positive mindset and sincere appreciation for life. In other words, I try to give them perspective through his experiences.

My work as a surgeon gives me a unique insight into the importance of perspective. Every day with my polytrauma cases, I meet people who suffer tremendous injuries, such as a worker who lost his hand from an accident on an oil rig, or a veterinarian who lost her fingers after getting attacked on the job. I see the unquestionable weight of trauma as my patients recount the events that led to their injury. The nature of our interactions often mutes whatever differences may exist in our values, beliefs, or behaviors. Medicine peels back our seemingly greatest differences to reveal our common humanity and mutual respect for life.

In medicine, my responsibility reaches beyond the physical realm to the psychological, emotional, social, and professional arenas of life. I need not only to surgically repair the physical injury itself but also to repair the invisible disabilities that accompany it. I strive to teach people never to give up no matter how severe or debilitating their circumstances.

During my residency program at the Mayo Clinic, our supervisors told us to tie our thumbs to our hands. I remember thinking, "Why? What does that accomplish?" After the exercise, I realized its purpose: to help us experience the challenges our patients underwent after surgery. It taught me just how difficult life can become without the use of our hands or upper extremity. The simple act of tying my shoe became nearly an impossible task. Multiply that across all the activities we automatically perform and take for granted, and the challenges of living become almost too difficult to bear.

I find my ability to connect essential to this responsibility. Connectedness enables me to cross the boundaries my patients self-construct against the external world. This means diagnosing their needs without asking them—telling a joke at just the right time, providing reassurances, relaying experiences to provide comfort, and so on. It allows me to help them see a world unrestricted by their injury and value what they didn't lose—the family sitting out in the waiting room, their remaining fingers or hand, and so on.

This brings me to the fifth outcome of connectedness: perspective, or seeing the world from a more informed, objective, and comprehensive point of view. Perspective enables us to fully appreciate life and the people surrounding us. It allows us to savor moments that usually pass unconsciously and enjoy the relationships we would otherwise take for granted. Perspective strips away our entitlements and overconfidence, and injects us with humility.

Perspective comes from connectedness and its many outcomes. The purpose we discover, the partnerships we create, the perseverance we experience, and the support we receive all contribute to a more well-rounded perspective that enables us to truly see the world and those around us. And it gives us a new and better outlook on life. At the same time, perspective also reinforces the other outcomes of connectedness. It helps us find our purpose, form partnerships, persevere, and find support.

Connectedness enables us to learn from others. It tells us how they experience the world around them, which helps to define how we should approach our interactions—whether offering support, advice, resistance, or persistence, and so on. Connectedness feeds our perspective much like a power cord fuels an appliance. Without it, we simply cannot acquire the perspective that accompanies an enriching life.

I often bring up Faruk in conversations with patients and health-care providers, as well as people I meet in a business context. He represents the standard of what we can accomplish in life through perspective. My patients listen with hope as I describe his journey, which gives proof that they can overcome their present circumstances and lead a rewarding life. My fellow practitioners relate his story to some of the exceptional cases they encounter. And my business partners stop to recognize what truly matters.

Perspective comes from people and their experiences. We will never have perspective without seeking to connect with others on a deeper level. Connectedness helps me gain perspective by putting me in contact with people who bring different experiences, backgrounds, and viewpoints. Before I met Faruk, I didn't know about the challenges of living as an orphan without the use of his hands. After our first encounter, I gained a glimpse into the world in which he lived, a glimpse that only became more complete and more nuanced over time. And as a result, I discovered someone who would forever change my perspective on life.

In my experience, I find that medicine naturally lends perspective. We discover stories of adversity that add meaning to our daily experiences and force us to consider what we naturally take for granted. Outside of health care, however, it often becomes more difficult to gain or maintain perspective. I find this especially true in business, where the frenetic pace of growing an enterprise and the desire to succeed come at the expense of forming the important connections that enable us to see and appreciate the needs of our employees, customers, and stakeholders. We tend to lose perspective rather than gain it, and our business suffers as a result.

This is not to say it takes tragedy or significant hardship in order to gain perspective. Adversity does accelerate the process, but we can also attain it by becoming more connected to those around us, considering the world through their eyes and experiences, and being cognizant that our point of view only constitutes a fraction of the subjectivity that exists.

I became successful as an entrepreneur in health care because I could relate to my patients and their experiences. I spent years observing all the anxiety and stress that accompanied an injury or illness, an experience that weighed significantly on patients and their family members. I understood that this experience often hindered the healing process. As a result, I designed a hospital that would provide not only excellent medical treatment but also the best experience for patients, considering the circumstances. In fact, I designed patient rooms to reflect what people would expect while staying at an upscale hotel. While many would call this unnecessary, it made a significant difference in bringing patients back to health. And I only knew how to design the quarters from my conversations with and observations of patients with whom I interacted. "If you could design this room, what would you want in it?" I asked. In every context of life, the seemingly smallest details can and often do make the greatest impact. I believed that if we could ease the burden of undergoing surgery and dealing with a medical condition, my patients would heal faster and better. In health care, we need to treat not only the condition but also the people most affected by it.

I carried this learning over to my endeavors in hospitality, where I sought to eliminate all the pain points travelers typically encounter and provide the experiences they want. And it continues to influence how I approach my work across industries. Essential to this understanding is the perspective I gain from meeting with people, learning about them, and appreciating their needs.

In my experience, the closer we become to people, the more perspective we gain, and vice versa.

The importance of perspective is not confined to medicine or entrepreneurship. It remains an essential condition in every industry and profession. The more we can connect with others, learn about them, and consider their points of view, the better able we become in collaborating with others and problem-solving in ways that create value. In my experience, the most successful people use connectedness to take a more informed perspective to their work, remain balanced, and successfully relate to people from all backgrounds.

Perspective remains one of the most important conditions for living a life of abundance. It enables us to understand the important forces at work in our society and culture. It teaches us to empathize with people of all diversities, engage in constructive dialogue, and challenge different points of view, not to silence them but to better understand them. In every way, perspective contributes to a more complete, fulfilling life for all of us who can attain it.

8

TRUST *through* CONNECTEDNESS

Melissa, one of my nurses, brought me a handwritten note, which I opened and read in the quiet of an exam room. Tucked in the envelope rested a photo of a man smiling and sitting on an empty stage. He held up a violin as if to celebrate the moments after winning an award.

> *Dear Dr. George,*
> *Thank you for giving me back my hand and my life. And thank you for talking me out of my stubbornness. I can't tell you how much it means to make music again.*
> *Warmly,*
> *Paul*

Several weeks before, Paul had visited the clinic for his hand consultation. It became quickly apparent that he distrusted the health-care system and its providers. He admitted to only visiting the clinic with his wife's encouragement, and because he could hardly tolerate the pain in his hand. Paul suffered from rheumatoid arthritis, and his condition worsened to the point he could no longer play the music he loved.

"I don't want surgery," he said, seconds after I introduced myself. I'd entered the exam room and taken a seat across from him. "I don't. I know you're going to tell me I should get surgery. I want to know what my options are."

"Fair enough. Let's take a look though," I said.

I took his hand and began examining it while asking questions about his work, life, and hobbies. I wanted to understand his condition while at the same time demonstrating my sincere interest in and attention to his world. And after several minutes, it seemed to work. Paul's shoulders loosened, and he started speaking more freely, abandoning the one-word answers he'd used at the start our conversation.

"Let's see your X rays," I said, turning on the illuminated viewer on the wall to show the black-and-white image of his hand. I used the image to explain his condition, the cause of his symptoms, and how his use of his hand factored into its current state. It provided visual support and anchored our conversation in the objective science of physiology and medicine. As a result, the discussion naturally moved to a place free of perceived bias and suspicion. Paul asked intelligent questions that showed his engagement and understanding of his health issue. "How exactly would an operation fix that?" he asked. Later, he inquired, "How long would it take before the pain in my hand would go away?"

I guided him through every step of the procedure and what he would experience. Yet I also presented his nonsurgical options, so he gained all the information needed to make an educated decision. At the end of our visit, I gave him my recommendation for surgery and talked through my reasoning. Surgery would provide him the best chance to regain normal hand function.

"Okay," he said. "Let's do the surgery."

Weeks later, Paul underwent his procedure, which proved successful. As his note showed, he experienced a full recovery.

As a physician, I encounter some patients who doubt my intentions or my ability to fix their health concerns. In these cases, I must actively build trust through a process that draws heavily on connectedness and the many actions and behaviors that support it. Paul's case is a good example.

My work in medicine gives me unique insight into the power of trust. Every day, I ask my patients to put their well-being in my hands and their confidence in my abilities. And while my credentials and reputation help toward this aim, they do not guarantee success of any kind. Building trust represents a challenging endeavor, especially since it must occur during the 15 minutes allotted to a consultation. In this time, I must work past the fears, anxieties, and barriers that prevent me from making the best diagnosis and recommendation. In other words, I must eliminate any second-guessing in a relationship that calls for mutual dependence. While my patients depend on my recommendations and care, I depend on their information and compliance with the course of action upon which we agree. I must also learn about my patients on a deeply personal level, and that means uncovering the details that live beyond the walls of the clinic and data contained in their medical records. And last, I need to demonstrate my competence, capability, and sincere commitment to their health and well-being.

I find that connectedness enhances my ability to establish a trusting relationship with my patients, who come from a variety of backgrounds and each bring unique circumstances that often complicate an interaction. Connectedness enables me to empathize with and relate to them and demonstrate this understanding verbally and nonverbally. I anticipate and address their concerns, make them the focus of the visit, listen to them actively and openly, and ask questions that show my attention to and understanding of who they are—not just as a patient but as a person and, in most cases, a professional. The latter is especially important since my recommendations may serve the person and come at the expense of the professional, or vice versa. For instance, my recommendation for a professional athlete may mean the end of a career but the continuation of a normal life. Or it may mean changing deeply ingrained behaviors to expand the longevity of a career. In these cases, my goal is to help my patients recognize a future beyond what they know and see, which often incites doubt, resistance, and rejection. Getting my patients to accept this reality is difficult, yet necessary, and trust rests at the core of navigating this delicate balance.

That brings me to the sixth outcome of connectedness: trust, or earning the confidence, belief, respect, and reliance of others. Trust lays the foundation of any meaningful, enduring relationship and remains incredibly important to every facet of life—whether raising kids, supporting a spouse, or leading and developing people, and so on. In my experience, the most successful people in life inspire others to trust them, while actively looking for people to trust in return.

When I think of helping others become successful, I find trust an essential force. Trust has enabled me to surround myself with a loving, devoted family, develop important relationships and professional acquaintances, and build and lead successful businesses comprised of talented, reliable, and committed individuals. In my experience, it represents the essence of "We."

Trust is an essential driver of success no matter our profession or industry. From entry-level professionals to senior executives, trust enables us to develop healthy working relationships with customers, collaborate successfully with colleagues, and gain the confidence of superiors. And the importance of trust only increases depending on our power and influence in an organization. As leaders, for instance, we must be able to build trust for others to follow us and buy into the direction we set. Those who follow us need not only trust in our ability to lead the organization, department, or team to a better place, but also believe in our commitment to protecting the greater interests of the collective and the individual members who contribute to it. At the same time, leaders need to create a culture of transparency that facilitates organizational engagement, commitment, and alignment.

Beyond medicine, I find trust especially important as an entrepreneur. It calls for getting others to commit to a journey that naturally entails significant hardship and certain risk, all without the guarantee of a return. At the same time, it requires creating the conditions to develop and sustain a trustworthy organization. Part of that comes from hiring the right people, yet it also comes from setting an example, keeping everyone accountable, and reinforcing the habits and behaviors that strengthen trust among employees and customers, partners, and other stakeholders.

In my experience, connectedness enhances our ability to build and sustain trust. It makes us more attentive to the needs and concerns of those around us. We become better listeners, more patient, and more inquisitive when it comes to the experiences of those with whom we meet. It also enables us to help others. By understanding people's context—including the reasoning behind their actions or inactions, decisions or indecisions—we truly begin to understand how we can help them.

As a result, we improve our chances of *actually* helping them, which only further strengthens their trust in us. Connectedness also enables us to establish full transparency and eliminate the skepticism, uncertainty, or confusion that comes when people believe we are withholding information. And last, connectedness feeds our purpose, leads to partnerships, solidifies our perseverance, gives us support, and strengthens our perspective. In other words, connectedness makes us successful in our chosen profession. Consequently, we naturally earn others' confidence in our ability to apply our knowledge, skills, and experience to whatever obstacles we encounter.

For Paul, I recognized that his frustration came from fear of losing something he cherished—his ability to play music. The prospect of losing an activity that defined him stoked his frustration and skepticism. For this reason, I chose to focus most of our visit on instruction, teaching him about his injury and shifting his decision-making from an emotional context to a logical one. Had I made my recommendation at the start of our encounter, he would have rejected it entirely. I would have confirmed what Paul initially expected from me and what fueled his distrust: my motives were focused on the transaction, not his well-being. It took careful guidance to earn his trust, and as a result, I could help him recapture a critical part of his life.

We need trust to form our most meaningful and enduring relationships. But we also need to trust ourselves. Connectedness enhances this process by showing us our strengths and weaknesses, values and beliefs, motivations and aspirations, and so on. Through deep introspection, we uncover our greatest skills and abilities, which introduces us to our purpose, bolsters our success, and increases our self-confidence. We become more certain of our ability to succeed no matter the circumstance and to endure hardship of any degree. As a result, we increase our chances of succeeding. And through this process, we also become more capable of developing and sustaining trusting relationships with others.

I cannot overstate the importance of trust in my life. And I believe its importance only continues to increase. In many ways, I see technology and instantaneous communication—social media, texting, emailing, etc.—as factors that often erode or impede our trust in one another. It only underscores the need to embrace connectedness and invest in human interaction. Once we do, we discover a life far more fulfilling than we previously imagined.

CONCLUSION

I never thought of writing a book. Rather, I thought of ways of capturing the remarkable stories of the people I encountered over the past 26 years of practicing medicine. They continue to fascinate me and keep me engaged in a profession that demands most of my time and attention.

I also wondered how I could keep record of my journey as an entrepreneur and the businesses I either built, helped build, or invested in. At the same time, I wanted to document the great minds I continued to meet across a variety of industries—experts in their field who exposed me to aspects of the world I didn't know. I sought to write about the many lessons I kept learning in business, which challenged me intellectually, and in an entirely different way than medicine.

Additionally, I wanted to help people—whether my patients or those I encountered in a business context—overcome a pattern of behavior I found detrimental to their personal and professional success, a pattern that, at the time, I couldn't quite articulate but could recognize existed. In many cases, this pattern made people ignore, reject, or resist opportunities for growth. I noticed it also made people neglect, constrain, or destroy their connections to others, even though they could help them live a more fulfilling life, at the very least in one context.

I talked to my father when the idea for this book came together. He spoke of the uniqueness of my work as a hand surgeon and serial entrepreneur.

"You must realize how contradictory your professions are," he'd said.

"How so?" I'd asked.

"Well, on the one hand, you're treating patients individually. Your focus is microscopic. On the other, you're scaling companies and reaching thousands of people in the process. Your focus is 40,000 feet from the ground. How do you balance them?"

I thought about his question for several days. How did I balance my work as a surgeon and entrepreneur? Medicine consumed most of my waking hours. Yet I managed to keep a successful marriage, stay close to my children, and grow businesses in several different industries that brought their own unique set of conditions, rules, and requirements for success.

Though I didn't know a name for it yet, I knew the answer as connectedness, what I embraced as a life force. And given what I'd observed in the numerous people I encountered through my work, I decided to write about this life philosophy. It became the impetus for this work.

Connectedness represents a lifestyle and mindset that determines how we engage with the external world. This includes how we interact with people, ideas, and perspectives. It refers to an active, ongoing state of living, not a fleeting episode or passive activity. At any moment in time, we either connect or disconnect, and we can vacillate between either state from one second to the next. In this book, I wrote about a lifestyle that actively remains in the connectedness realm for at least most of the time.

Connectedness doesn't simply refer to the connections we make with people but also those we form by connecting parties that otherwise wouldn't meet without our help—and do so for their mutual benefit.

In my experience, connectedness enables us to overcome the obstacles and problems created by a mindset of "Me versus We"—specifically, a tendency to seek absolute independence personally or professionally, believe our destiny is determined by past events or present circumstances, and let a win-lose mindset dictate our actions, a belief that says someone must lose for us to gain. Connectedness enables us to see past and think beyond these barriers and recognize that the people we meet, ideas we encounter, and perspectives we consider make us stronger and represent the vehicle for creating the life we want for ourselves, our family, and others.

In this book, I don't attempt to provide a formula for embracing a mindset of connectedness. I don't believe a standard, step-by-step approach exists. Rather, I believe connectedness varies by individual, depending on his or her circumstances, profession, etc. Still, I believe it requires many of the fundamental principles explored in this book, which we can all attain.

I instead chose to explore six fundamental outcomes of connectedness to show what remains possible for anyone who embraces this life force. Those outcomes include purpose, partnerships, perseverance, support, perspective, and trust. And each contributes uniquely and similarly to living a fulfilling and abundant life.

As we explored, I define purpose as discovering how and where to focus our passions, interests, and talents to create shared, meaningful value. I discovered my purpose of practicing medicine through a journey of continual experimentation, active engagement with people and ideas, and self-introspection. As a result, I transformed—and continue to change—people's lives for the better. At the same time, I discovered my purpose of entrepreneurship through a similar journey, one that exposed me to a broad spectrum of people, ideas, and perspectives before I realized my true talent and interest for building businesses. This taught me that we never truly have only one purpose in life. And we cannot discover it overnight. Rather, it takes time to find our purpose, and even after realizing it, we may find others in the future.

I believe connectedness helps accelerate the process, teaching us early on where we can create the most value and feel most fulfilled. It helps us discover the opportunities that remain unseen in the potential connections surrounding us. Importantly, connectedness feeds our purpose, which enhances our desire to connect and leads to a life of abundance that creates value for everyone in the equation.

Partnerships represent the second outcome of connectedness. They are lasting relationships, loyalty, and sources for new ideas, perspectives, and opportunities. Partnerships often come as a result of our purpose, because when we embrace where we can succeed, seek to benefit others, and become people oriented, we cultivate truly rewarding and sustainable partnerships, which remain our strongest and most enduring asset. In my experience, embracing connectedness enables us to discover partners who share our passion and vision.

Partnerships exist in many different forms—whether our family, business partners, professional connections, or peers. They truly enable us to expand our knowledge and perspective of the world around us. And they reinforce our ability to connect with and establish other partnerships in the future. In fact, I find that partnerships enable us to form the important connections that stimulate us intellectually, socially, and emotionally.

The third outcome of connectedness is perseverance—the ability to overcome adversity and succeed through hardship. When we look at success in whatever form, we tend to overlook the significant sacrifice, hard work, and commitment it took to reach that position in life. Yet hardship exists in every context; we can't avoid or ignore it. We all face adversity in one form or another, often throughout our lives. What differentiates those of us who are successful is our ability to persevere and overcome challenges.

The most successful people in business willingly invite risk, stress, and challenge into their lives, knowing the rewards justify them. And they stay unyielding no matter how many times they experience failure. At the same time, the most successful entrepreneurs—and people in general—accept that opportunities don't always work out. And rather than cling to them, or become discouraged when they don't come to fruition, they accept this reality and move on. They recognize that their greatest asset resides in their partnerships, not in academic tests, degrees, business deals, etc. And as a result, they win more opportunities than they lose.

Support signifies the fourth outcome of connectedness. This includes developing a team of trustworthy people who share our passion and contribute to our purpose.

While partnerships and support share many similarities, I chose to treat them separately. I generally refer to partnerships as relationships that exist on a mutual plane, such as a partnership with a spouse, customer, fellow entrepreneur, or business partner who maintains a degree of separation from an enterprise. On the other hand, I refer to support as a system comprised of individuals who directly contribute to our organization and mission—for example, people working for us. The more connected we become, the more we can find the right people to support our goals in life, and the more we can help nurture their aspirations and needs.

Success requires great individual accomplishment. We can't succeed without performing our best. Yet we also can't attain any noteworthy accomplishment without the support of a collective team of people working in concert toward a shared vision. The success of an enterprise doesn't come from one person's intellect or knowledge but from the collective wisdom produced by an organization of people bringing unique talents and expertise to the enterprise.

The fifth outcome of connectedness, perspective, requires us to see the world from a more informed, objective, and comprehensive point of view. This outcome allows us to fully appreciate life and the people around us. Perspective enables us to consciously appreciate the experiences and people we otherwise wouldn't. In this way, it keeps us humble and not overconfident or entitled.

Perspective comes from connectedness and its many outcomes. Purpose, partnerships, perseverance, and support all contribute to a more complete perspective on life that enables us to appreciate the world around us. It gives us a new and better outlook on life. And it reinforces the other outcomes of connectedness.

Perspective also comes from people and their experiences. We cannot attain perspective without connecting with others on a deep, meaningful level. It teaches us to relate to people from all walks of life, interact with them, and challenge ideas and points of view different from our own.

The sixth and last outcome of connectedness is trust. Trust means earning the confidence, belief, and respect of others. It lays the foundation of any meaningful, enduring relationship and is incredibly important in all contexts. While its importance may vary slightly depending on our circumstances, it remains essential to finding success and living a life of abundance. In a professional context, trust enables us to develop healthy, productive relationships with customers, colleagues, and superiors. And its importance only increases as we experience success and attain more seniority in any organization. Leaders, for instance, need to inspire the trust of those following them. At the same time, they must also create the conditions to develop a trustworthy team, department, or company. This calls for teaching, mentoring, and holding others accountable in a manner that enhances transparency and facilitates engagement, motivation, and alignment.

The six outcomes of connectedness do not come in any order. Rather, I believe they are self-reinforcing, meaning they contribute to and strengthen one another. Purpose leads to partnerships, which bolsters our perseverance, strengthens our support, enhances our perspective, and invigorates our ability to inspire and invest trust in others. The same is true for any of the other five outcomes. For example, our ability to inspire trust enables us to discover our purpose, form partnerships, persevere, build a sustainable support system, and attain perspective. However, none of these outcomes are possible without a full commitment to connectedness.

My goal in writing this book is not to lecture or tell people how they should live their lives. I simply want to present what has truly made mine fulfilling. I seek to expose people of all ages and walks to a mindset that can help anyone achieve success—personally and professionally. One subset is aspiring entrepreneurs. My goal is to show them that they can build successful businesses, but only by investing in the people they encounter. Additionally, I hope to help them realize their full potential by discrediting the business axiom "Stay within your knowledge base." I believe entrepreneurs succeed when they find and partner with experts they can trust in the industries they want to enter. Had I confined myself to what I knew, medicine, I wouldn't be nearly as successful or fulfilled as I am today.

A second group is new and existing physicians. My aim is to illustrate that they can succeed in health care and business, yet it requires meeting and investing in people who can help them. That means recognizing that success in medicine is not the same as achievement in business. Successful physician-entrepreneurs recognize this and surround themselves with brilliant people who bring the needed talent and expertise to thrive in business. And rather than constrain them, these entrepreneurs empower them and concede key responsibilities while holding them accountable.

To everyone reading this book, I hope I have at least challenged your existing beliefs. I hope I have changed your perspective and inspired you to adopt a new mindset and approach to your personal and professional endeavors.

CITATIONS

Constantino, Tor. "Five Leadership Lessons from Steve Jobs." *Michael Hyatt.* November 4, 2011. Accessed October 24, 2018. https://michael-hyatt.com/five-leadership-lessons-from-steve-jobs/.

Plumer, Brad. "Only 27 percent of college grads have a job related to their major." *The Washington Post.* May 20, 2013. Accessed October 10, 2018. https://www.washingtonpost.com/news/wonk/wp/2013/05/20/only-27-percent-of-college-grads-have-a-job-related-to-their-major/?noredirect=on&utm_term=.b924a3431642.

INDEX